Journey into China

Natural Wonders in China

Liu Ying

translation by Zhou Xiaozheng

JOURNEY INTO CHINA

Counsellor: Cai Wu
General Director: Li Bing
Chief Editors: Guo Changjian & Li Xiangping
Deputy Chief Editor: Wu Wei

图书在版编目（CIP）数据

自然之旅：英文/刘莹著；周效政译.—北京：五洲传播出版社，2007.8
（中国之旅）(2008.5重印)
ISBN 978-7-5085-1104-7

I. 自…
II. ①刘… ②周…
III. 自然地理－简介－中国－英文
IV. P942

中国版本图书馆CIP数据核字（2007）第064527号

NATURAL WONDERS IN CHINA

Author: Liu Ying
Translator: Zhou Xiaozheng
Planner: Feng Lingyu
Project Director: Deng Jinhui
Executive Editor: Xu Weiran
Art Director: Tian Lin
Publisher: China Intercontinental Press (6 Beixiaomachang, Lianhuachi Donglu, Haidian District, Beijing 100038, China)
Printer: Beijing Picture in Picture Printing Co., Ltd.
Tel: 86-10-58891281
Website: www.cicc.org.cn
Edition: Aug. 2007, 1st edition, May. 2008, 2nd print run
Format: 787×1092mm 1/16
Signatures: 10.5
Words: 45,000
Print Run: 7001–14,000
Price: RMB 96.00 (yuan)

Contents

THE SPLENDOR OF CHINA'S NATURAL BEAUTY 5

GREAT MOUNTAINS 9

9 *Mount Qomolangma: On Top of the World*
13 *Mount Namjagbarwa: A Myth in the Clouds*
16 *Mount Taishan: Head of the Five Great Mountains*
20 *The Yellow Mountain: A Mountain of Art*
24 *The Meili Snow Mountain: Honor Guard of the Snow God*
28 *The Danxia Mountain: A Wonderland of Red Rocks*
31 *The Rongbuk Glacier: A City of Ice and Snow*
34 *The Hailuogou Glacier: Grand Ice Fall From Heaven*

RIVERS AND LAKES 37

37 *The Yangtze River: China's Artery*
42 *The Yellow River: Cradle of the Chinese Civilization*
46 *The Three Gorges: Beyond Time and Space*
50 *The Three Parallel Rivers: Dancing Mountains and Rivers*
56 *The Kanas Lake: Unparalleled Beauty*
60 *The Namco Lake: Heavenly Lake on the Plateau*
65 *The Qinghai Lake: A Sea in the Heart of the Land*
69 *Jiuzhaigou: A Colorful Painting*

DESERTS AND GRASSLANDS 73

73 *The Taklimakan Desert: Graveyard of Ancient Civilizations*
76 *The Badain Jaran Desert: On Top of All Deserts*
79 *The Hulun Buir Grassland: A Thousand-Year-Old Idyllic Song*
83 *Bayanbulak: A Swan Lake in the Embrace of Snowy Mountains*
86 *Zoige: A Highland Jade*
90 *The Yellow River Delta Wetland: The Youngest Soil*

GEOLOGICAL WONDERS 95

95 *The Lunan Stone Forest: Natural Stone Sculptures*
99 *Wulingyuan: Thousands of Cliffs in Competition With Each Other*
103 *The Yuanmou Clay Forest: A Golden Palace of Gods*
107 *Zhijin Cave: An Underground Treasure House*
110 *Wu'erhe: Residence of Devils*
113 *Guilin: A Beautiful Legend of a Thousand Years*
116 *The Yellow Dragon Ravine: A Huge Dragon Hidden in Deep Mountains*
119 *Yeliu: A Sculpture Park on the Coast*

COLORFUL ECO-SYSTEMS 123

123 *The Tropical Rain Forest in Xishuangbanna: A Wild Jungle*
127 *The Bamboo Sea in Southern Sichuan: A Tranquil World of Bamboo*
130 *The Diverse-Leaf Poplar Forest in Luntai: Heroic Trees in the Desert*
135 *The Changbai Mountain Forest: Virgin Forest in North China*
138 *The Giant Panda Habitat in Sichuan: Homeland of the Giant Pandas*
142 *Hoh Xil Highland Wildlife Habitat: A Paradise in No Man's Land*
145 *Shennongjia: A Mystic Haven for Wildlife*

BLUE TERRITORY 149

149 *Chengshantou: A Battlefield of Land and Sea*
153 *The South China Sea Islands: China's Pearl Necklace*

APPENDIX: CHINA'S GENERAL NATURAL CONDITIONS 157

The Splendor of China's Natural Beauty

China is located in east Eurasia and on the Pacific west coast, covering 9.6 million sq. km of land and 3 million sq. km of sea. It stretches across four time zones east to west and covers 5,500 km north to south, while the elevation gap between its highest peak and lowest point reaches nearly 9,000 meters. The great geographical differences and contrasts have made this land both dynamic and magnificent. There are snow-capped mountains, glaciers, evergreen rain forests, desolate gobis and deserts, vibrant lakes and coasts, spectacular valleys and waterfalls, and boundless grasslands and wetlands... In China, almost all types of natural scenery that exist in the world can be found, and this book intends to help you learn something about its beauty.

You will find masculine beauty here–in the world's highest peak, Mount Qomolangma, in the world's tallest mountains, the Himalayas, and in the Hailuogou Glacier, which has a fall of more than 1,000 meters.

You will find wild beauty here–in the ferocious winds and sweeping sandstorms in the Taklimakan Desert, that can eclipse the sun in seconds and that has mercilessly buried numerous ancient civilizations, and in the no man's land on the Hoh Xil Plateau, where Tibetan antelopes, wild yaks and Tibetan wild donkeys gallop freely and elegantly, although the air they breathe contains less than half the oxygen in the air at sea level.

You will find feminine beauty here–in the picturesque mountains and serene rivers of Guilin in Guangxi, in the Bayanbulak grasslands in the hinterland of Xinjiang's Tianshan Mountains, which is the world's largest swan habitat, and in Jiuzhaigou in Sichuan's mountainous area, which has an

abundance of lakes in a multitude of colors.

You will also find mysterious beauty here—in the "lake monster" of Kanas and the legendary "Big Foot" in the virgin forest of Shennongjia, in the unusually shaped natural stone sculptures on Taiwan's Yeliu Coast, as well as in the karst caves that exist in many regions of the country, which are unexplored underground labyrinths housing unknown treasures.

1	2	5	6
3	4		

1.The Shuzheng Waterfall
2.The terrace paddy field in Yunnan
3.The Poyang Lake
4.The coastline
5.The Huoshao Mountain in Xinjiang
6.Sunflower in Xinjiang

With its long history, huge population and vast territory, China has nurtured a splendid culture. For thousands of years, human activities have had a far-reaching impact on the natural environment and added a profoundly human touch to the mountains, rivers, lakes and seas. For example, stone inscription on the cliffs and crags of Mount Taishan has never ceased over the past 2,000 years, leaving a vivid legacy of China's development. The Three Gorges on the Yangtze River have attracted so much attention from Chinese poets and artists of all times that they could be called a "gallery of poetry and painting." And the Yellow Mountain, famed as the "miniature garden of God" for its fascinating landscape, has inspired the emergence of new schools of poetry and painting, thus leaving an indelible mark on traditional Chinese culture.

It is impossible to make a full presentation of China's natural beauty in the limited space of this book. While this book could only name a few of the most beautiful places in China, all natural wonders in the country are open to friends from all over the world.

Great Mountains

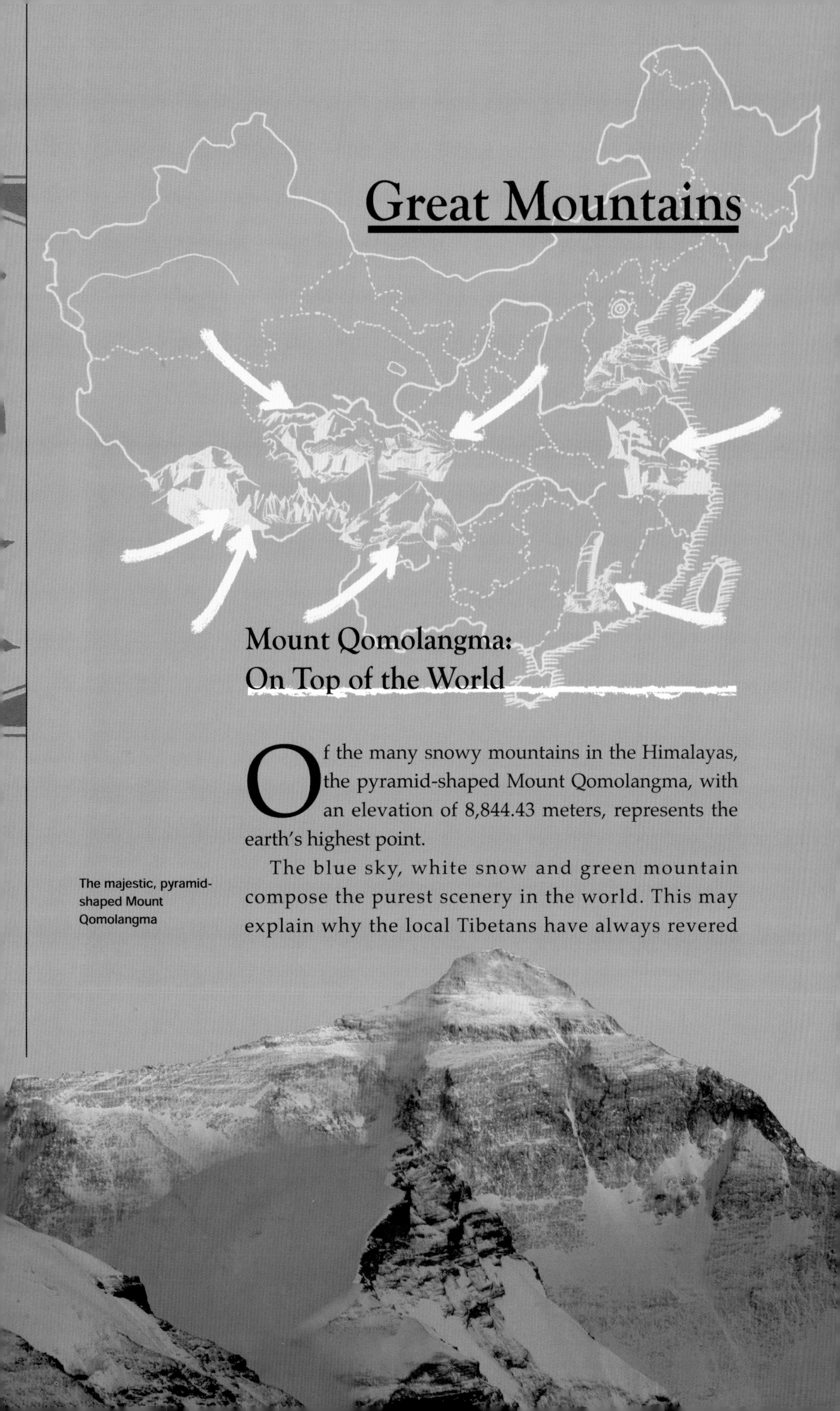

Mount Qomolangma: On Top of the World

Of the many snowy mountains in the Himalayas, the pyramid-shaped Mount Qomolangma, with an elevation of 8,844.43 meters, represents the earth's highest point.

The blue sky, white snow and green mountain compose the purest scenery in the world. This may explain why the local Tibetans have always revered

The majestic, pyramid-shaped Mount Qomolangma

The beautiful Mount Qomolangma has an everlasting charm, because it is the closest point to heaven on earth.

Mount Qomolangma as a "sacred goddess."

Mount Qomolangma is located on China's southwest borders, with its southern slope in Nepal and northern slope in China's Tibet Autonomous Region. The supreme height of Mount Qomolangma is a result of the collision of two major continental plates: the Indian landmass collided with Asia, which resulted in the world's highest and largest plateau, the Qinghai-Tibet Plateau. The Himalayas, which happened to be on the boundary of the two continental plates, was the aftermath of the enormous colliding force, with Mount Qomolangma being its highest peak. Within an area of 20 sq. km around Mount Qomolangma, a wide array of tall, snowy mountains can be found; more than 40 have an elevation exceeding 7,000 meters.

Mount Qomolangma looks most beautiful at daybreak when the sky is clear. Upon sunrise, Mount Qomolangma receives the first ray of light because of its height, while neighboring snowy mountains are still enveloped in darkness. With the white snow and black rocks all bathed in golden sunlight, Mount Qomolangma appears like a god in golden attire, radiating beams atop a vast snowy land. In the Tibetan language, qomo means "goddess" while langma means "third." The locals believe that Mount Qomolangma is the third eldest among four high peaks, or four goddesses in the region; hence, its name.

It is not easy to have a close look at the true face of this mountain. On the north side, the place closest to the peak and still suitable for human activity is located in Tingri County of Tibet, which is more than 6,000 meters above sea level and which now serves as the base camp for mountain climbers. The weather here is extremely inhospitable to humans, and the oxygen level in the air is less than half that at sea level. Even in summer, the region could be struck by hurricane-level snowstorms, the sunlight eclipsed in seconds. As similar sights could only be found in the North and South Poles, Mount Qomolangma is also called "the third pole of the world." Nonetheless, such harsh natural conditions have never kept people from Mount Qomolangma, which, as the world's highest peak, has always been a mecca for climbers across the world. Since the 18th century, numerous teams of climbers have come to its base in an attempt to conquer it. From the 1920s to 1930s, British explorers tried seven times to climb from the north slope, but all failed. Some even lost their lives.

It was not until May 1953 that mankind first left its footprints on the top of the world. New Zealand

It is very difficult to climb the steep Mount Qomolangma.

mountaineer Edmund Hillary and his sherpa assistant Tenzing Norgay made history as they overcame all kinds of hardship in climbing to the top of Mount Qomolangma from the south slope. In 1960, a Chinese climbing team ascended the peak from the north slope, opening a new climbing route for mountaineers worldwide.

Mount Qomolangma has an everlasting charm, because it is the closest point to heaven on earth.

Mount Namjagbarwa: A Myth in the Clouds

A lofty snow peak, Mount Namjagbarwa got its name from a Tibetan word used to describe it in the Tibetan epic King Gesar, which literally means "a spear piercing the sky."

With clouds and mist surrounding its peak, river valleys at its base and dense forest all around, Mount Namjagbarwa has been selected as "the prettiest peak in China" by scientists, explorers and climbers in the country.

Located in Nyingchi Prefecture southeast to the Tibet Autonomous Region, Mount Namjagbarwa has an elevation of 7,782 meters and is the 15th highest peak in the world. The distance between the top and the foot of Mount Namjagbarwa is just 2 km, but drastic seasonal contrasts—from a freezing winter to a sweltering summer —can be experienced, and a colorful world featuring both white snow and evergreen plants can be seen.

Mount Namjagbarwa seems too shy to show its face, as it always hides itself in thick clouds. Only those with utmost sincerity can look at its true face.

Mount Namjagbarwa is snow-capped year-round, and

below the snow line grows dark-green alpine vegetation. Further below are small clusters of shrubs, the prettiest of which are the light-purple alpine rhododendron and pink polyanthus. The shrubland is followed by the boreal forest or Taiga, where a large number of sturdy firs grow. On the lower brink of the boreal forest are trees with broader leaves, as well as camphor trees with a unique fragrance and various rhododendra. The forest turns denser as the base of the mountain draws closer, while tropical plants such as bananas extend their huge leaves in a hot, humid environment typical of a rain forest. With

Thanks to its drastic fall, Mount Namjagbarwa boasts a variety of animal and plant species and has earned the fame as "a natural museum of mountain vegetation in the world."

its drastic fall, Mount Namjagbarwa seems to be a master magician with several different faces to show the world at the same time. No wonder it has earned the fame as "a natural museum of mountain vegetation in the world."

Mount Namjagbarwa seems too shy to show its face, as it always hides itself in thick clouds. An ancient mythology may explain the reason. It says that long, long ago two gods were assigned to guard southeast Tibet; they were brothers, Namjagbarwa and Gyalha Bairi. The younger brother, Gyalha Bairi, was so handsome, strong and accomplished that the elder brother, Namjagbarwa, murdered him out of jealousy. Later, both brothers transformed into the mountains. Mount Gyalha Bairi has a round top, because the poor, younger brother's head had been chopped off by the jealous, older brother, while Mount Namjagbarwa hides itself in clouds and mist year-round, the elder brother being extremely ashamed of his own sin.

Blocked from public sight, Mount Namjagbarwa appears to be a mysterious wonderland that can only be reached in a dream. The local Tibetans say that only those with utmost sincerity can look at its true face. However, some British explorers once waited for more than a month at the base but still couldn't see it clearly. According to the explanation of geographers, Mount Namjagbarwa stands next to the Yarlung Zangbo River Grand Canyon, which serves as a channel for the north movement of the humid air from the Indian Ocean. As a result, high mountains along the canyon are often shrouded in clouds and mist.

Seen from its base, Mount Namjagbarwa resembles an attired god with white clouds as his belt. The mountain peak always hides in a sea of clouds, only revealing itself for a short moment occasionally. The local Tibetans believe that a road to heaven exists atop this mountain, and that the immortals are on their way to the heavenly palace whenever the mountain peak is densely shrouded by clouds.

Mount Taishan: Head of the Five Great Mountains

With an elevation of 1,545 meters, the Jade Emperor Peak is the highest peak of Mount Taishan which many Chinese monarchs had ascended to hold the "*Fengshan*" rituals and pay homage to heaven and earth.

In history, Mount Taishan is always seen as the most famous mountain of the country. Although it is not very high—with an elevation of merely 1,500 meters —Mount Taishan has assumed extremely important status in Chinese history and culture. Although it is well-known that Mount Qomolangma is the highest peak in the world from a geographical perspective, Mount Taishan stands tallest in China from a cultural perspective.

Located in central Shandong Province, Mount Taishan is the highest mountain in the vast region along the lower reaches of the Yellow River. Compared with the plains and low hills surrounding it, Mount Taishan is overwhelmingly dominant and thus boasts an all-conquering magnificence. The region where Mount

All kinds of stone carvings can be spotted on the rocks along the mountain path in Mount Taishan. The photo shows one of the most famous stone inscriptions which reads "Head of the Five Great Mountains."

Taishan lies was one of the cradles of the ancient Chinese civilization, and the mountain used to be a key shelter for the ancestors.

Mount Taishan was also called "Daishan" or "Daizong" in ancient times. In ancient Chinese, the word "Dai" means "great," so the literal meaning of "Daishan" is "the great mountain." In the eyes of the Chinese ancestors, Mount Taishan was of a supreme height unmatchable by any other mountain; this lay a solid foundation for Mount Taishan to gradually assume a leading role in all Chinese mountains. Covering 426 sq. km, Mount Taishan is a large range consisting of more than 100 mountains and hills, with the Jade Emperor Peak as its highest peak. There are also 98 cliffs and ridges, 102 creeks and ravines in the mountain range. Mount Taishan boasts a beautiful landscape and climbers enjoy a visual feast all the way to the mountain peak. Standing on top of Mount Taishan and gazing around, with no obstacles to block the view, it is natural to have the feeling of "standing on top of the world."

A significant feature of Mount Taishan is the perfect combination of natural scenery and cultural heritage. Mount Taishan lies in the eastern part of the country, while the ancient Chinese worshipped "East," seeing it as the place for sunrise, seasonal changes and the arrival of spring. Therefore, Mount Taishan became the only famous mountain in Chinese history that had served as the site for the grand ceremony of "*Feng Shan*," or worship of heaven and earth by ancient emperors. For many generations, the mountain had been a top attraction for kings and emperors, poets and writers, who left behind numerous cultural relics and historic sites. Apart from ancient temples and statues, the mountain also boasts more than 2,000 cliff inscriptions of Chinese calligraphy, among which the four-character inscription "*Wu Yue Du Zun*" (Head of the Five Great Mountains) has now become the mountain's logo.

The "Five Great Mountains" refer to five mountains that have enjoyed great fame in China since ancient times, namely Mount Taishan (the eastern great mountain), Mount Huashan (the western great mountain), Mount Songshan (the central great mountain), Mount Hengshan (of Hunan Province, the southern great mountain), and Mount Hengshan (of Shanxi Province, the northern great mountain). The origin of the "Five Great Mountains" can be traced back to the time when ancient Chinese worshipped major mountains and rivers. The Chinese mythology says that after the demise of the world-creating god Pan Gu, his head and limbs turned into the "Five Great Mountains." In terms of altitude, Mount Taishan ranks just third among the "Five Great Mountains," and many more mountains are higher than it across the country. Then how has it become the head of the five great mountains and also assumed the leading role in all Chinese mountains? A main factor is the culture of "*Feng Shan*" in China. Since emperors of successive feudal dynasties went to Mount Taishan to

"The Eighteen Bends" is the steepest section of the mountain path leading to the top of Mount Taishan. With a total of more than 1,600 steps, it looks like a ladder stretching down from the heaven.

hold the solemn ritual of worshipping heaven and earth, the mountain itself also assumed the lofty status as a symbol of national prosperity and ethnic unity. It was also regarded as a symbol of Oriental civilization and a manifestation of the ancient Chinese thought of "the unity of human and nature."

Many ancient and rare trees can be found on Mount Taishan, including six cypress trees planted by emperors of the Han Dynasty, which are now more than 2,100 years old. There are also pagoda trees that were planted some 1,300 years ago and pine trees dating back 500 years. In 1987, the United Nations granted Mount Taishan the double honor as a site of both world natural and cultural heritage.

The Yellow Mountain: A Mountain of Art

The Yellow Mountain assumes a very special status in China's history and culture, and was reputed as being "the most beautiful mountain in China" for a long period of time.

Located in the southern mountainous region of Anhui Province, the Yellow Mountain was also called "Mount *Yishan*" in ancient times. It is said that the legendary common ancestor of the Chinese, the Great Emperor of Xuan Yuan, meditated and performed magic here until he became immortal and joined the ranks of celestial beings. The Great Emperor of Xuan Yuan was also known as the Yellow Emperor, so an emperor of the Tang Dynasty (618–907) ordered Mount Yishan to be renamed the "Yellow Mountain" in memory of the country's common ancestor.

The Yellow Mountain boasts a host of marvelous peaks, 72 of which are of great renown. Among them 36 are of bigger size and look steep and magnificent, while the other half are smaller but appear charming and lovely.

The odd-shaped pine trees, unusual rocks and sea of clouds at the Yellow Mountain.

Each of the peaks has a large quantity of unusual rocks, which exist in tens of thousands of fantastic shapes.

Co-existing with the wonderful peaks and unusual rocks are the famous "Yellow Mountain Pines," which can be found everywhere—from the cliffs to the summits. With stretching, twisting branches, flat crowns, and dark green leaves that are short, thick and dense, these pine trees are deeply rooted in the cracks of the rocks and have managed to survive in the bare soil between the cracks. Standing firm on the cliffs or steep slopes and braving gusts and blizzards, the Yellow Mountain Pines have demonstrated a persistent, strong life force, thus becoming synonymous with "endurance" and "perseverance" in the Chinese culture. People who visit the Yellow Mountain not only enjoy its charming beauty, but gain spiritual revelation and inspiration.

If rocks and pines are the bones and flesh of the Yellow Mountain, then the sea of clouds is where the grace and elegance of the Yellow Mountain lie. When the clouds and mists accumulate, the body of the Yellow Mountain is enshrouded in a white sea, with only the high peaks still apparent. Watching the peaks disappear and emerge from the sea of clouds is like being in a dreamland. During the moments of sunrise and sunset, the sea of clouds looks even more brilliant with a spectrum of amazing colors.

The Yellow Mountain is blessed with a mixture of beauty that can be found in its mountain scenery: marvelous peaks, unusual rocks, pine trees, waterfalls, a sea of clouds and rosy sunrays. After touring the Yellow Mountain, Xu Xiake, a renowned Chinese traveler of the Ming Dynasty (1368–1644), wrote the famous verses: "One shall see no other mountains after seeing the Five Great Mountains, but after returning from the Yellow Mountain one will even lose interest in any of the Great Mountains." Xu's poem indicates that after touring the Yellow Mountain, one will no longer be impressed by the sight of any other mountains in the country.

The beautiful scenery of the Yellow Mountain has inspired the artistic creation of poets and painters for

The Welcoming Pine is a typical representative of the pine trees on the Yellow Mountain. With two major branches stretching out for 7.6 meters on both sides, the pine looks like a hospitable host opening his arms to warmly greet both domestic and overseas guests.

A sea of clouds has added more charm to the unusual peaks and grotesque rocks on the Yellow Mountain. The landscape embodies the essence of traditional Chinese landscape painting, even inspiring the birth of a new painting school—the Yellow Mountain Painting School.

"Monkey Watching the Sea"—one of the most renowned unusual rocks on the Yellow Mountain.

generations, and the Yellow Mountain itself has become the most described and eulogized mountain in China's art history. Incomplete statistics show that in the 1,200 years between the mid-Tang Dynasty and late Qing Dynasty, Chinese poets wrote more than 20,000 works of poetry to sing the praise of the Yellow Mountain. In Chinese painting, the landscape of the Yellow Mountain has also been a major influence on the development of China's traditional landscape painting, even inspiring the birth of a new painting school—the Yellow Mountain Painting School, which focuses on the landscape of the Yellow Mountain and aims to reflect the mountain's graceful nature.

Today, the Yellow Mountain remains one of the leading tourist attractions in China. In 1990, it was listed by the United Nations as a site of world natural and cultural heritage.

The Meili Snow Mountain: Honor Guard of the Snow God

The Meili Snow Mountain is on the boundary of Yunnan Province and Tibet Autonomous Region. It ranks first among the eight sacred mountains in the Tibetan region, and is also the highest mountain in Yunnan. The highest peak of the Meili Snow Mountain, the Kawagabo Peak, has an elevation of 6,740 meters. In the Tibetan language, Kawagabo means "god of the snow mountain." Around the Kawagabo Peak are 13 mountains whose altitudes exceed 6,000 meters. They are called the "13 princes peaks." These peaks all look magnificent and elegant, just like a guard of honor of the legendary Snow God.

The magnificence of the Meili Snow Mountain mainly arises from its huge fall, which is 4,702 meters from the summit Kawagabo to the convergence of the Lancang River (China's fifth largest river that flows across the foot of the Meili Snow Mountain) and Mingyong River, resulting in the formation of the precipitous Meili Grand Canyon.

Due to the huge fall, the climatic conditions in the Meili Snow Mountain change drastically according to the altitude: the high peaks above the snowline are snow-capped year-long and are often shrouded in clouds

The "13 princes peaks," each with an altitude of more than 6,000 meters, line up in a magnificent array and stay close to each other.

and mist, while below the snowline exist the alpine meadow, alpine shrubland and dense forest. Climbing the Meili Snow Mountain, the change of four seasons can be experienced in one day and different weather can be encountered in just a 5-km walk. The complicated and treacherous weather at Meili has led to a boom of biological species, with many rare and precious herbal plants, such as matsutake, fritillary and cordyceps sinensis, growing in the mountain. Meili is also a paradise for wild animals, accommodating such rare and endangered species as leopard, lesser panda and red deer.

Many types of glaciers can be found at Meili, with the Mingyong Glacier being the most famous. The Mingyong Glacier flows down Kawagabo Peak and stretches for 12 km on the Meili Snow Mountain. It winds through the mountain valley until reaching the forest belt at an elevation of over 2,600 meters, thus becoming China's lowest glacier in terms of altitude and latitude. Only at Meili can such a wonderful experience be had: standing under a blossoming azalea tree to view a vast glacier nearby.

A low-latitude glacier not only creates beautiful landscape, but also moves rapidly. Due to its topography, the Meili Snow Mountain each year witnesses great snowfall and melting snow, prompting the glaciers to move at a fast pace. Therefore, each year more avalanches occur at Meili than at any other place, posing a great threat to mountain climbers.

The Meathmu Peak and a highland village. The Meathmu Peak is the prettiest of the "13 princes peaks" and thus reputed as a "beauty peak" of the Meili Snow Mountain.

The Meili Snow Mountain has been ruthless to mountaineers and added a dark chapter to the world's climbing history late in the last century. In January 1991, a collaborative team of climbers from China and Japan tried to ascend Kawagabo Peak but were forced to give up due to a sudden, heavy snowfall. However, on their way back to the No. 3 camp at the 5,100-meter altitude point, the team encountered a major avalanche and all 17 members, including six Chinese and 11 Japanese, were killed; this marked the second worst disaster in world climbing history. Later, a monument dedicated

Scripture streamers flutter in the wind at the foot of the Meili Snow Mountain.

to the team was erected near the Meili Snow Mountain, just opposite Kawagabo Peak. To date, Kawagabo Peak remains a virgin peak that has never been conquered by man.

The Danxia Mountain: A Wonderland of Red Rocks

Red rocks, green trees and rosy clouds in the sky—all these form a wonderful scene at the Danxia Mountain, particularly at dawn and dusk.

Located in north Guangdong Province, the Danxia Mountain mainly consists of red sandstone and features a unique landform of red rocks and cliffs. Geologists have named this type of landform after the mountain, the Danxia landform. More than 700 other places in China feature the same landform, but Danxia Mountain is the most beautiful and most representative of all.

As long as 1,500 years ago, the Danxia Mountain had already been noticed by the ancient Chinese, who in their poems described the mountain as "having a red color as bright as the morning and evening glow." In the

The Male Symbol Stone

The Female Symbol Stone

stretching red hills are numerous large and small stone peaks, castles, walls and bridges—all in different shapes and all spectacular.

The Danxia Mountain hills have their own characteristics: a flat top and steep cliffs on one side, but, opposite the cliffs, gentle slopes. The slopes are mostly covered by flourishing vegetation, while the cliffs abound with bare, red rocks. The unique appearance of the hills has enabled the Danxia Mountain to display both masculine and feminine beauty. Facing the cliffs is like seeing the rocky cliffs, several hundred meters tall, as magnificent pillars, holding up the sky. Observing the mountain from afar, however, lends a gentle, warm feeling from the soft curves of the mountaintop and the slopes.

The unique red rocks of the Danxia Mountain came into being some 100 million years ago, when the place was an inland basin. The rocks around the basin broke and piled up, and due to the hot, dry climate dominating the region at that time, some substances in the rocks were oxygenated and turned rusty red. Over a period of 30 million years, the sediments in the basin gradually formed the red sandstone seen today. Later, as a result of the movement of the earth crust, the basin was lifted and became a mountainous region, while the cutting and erosion effect of flowing water contributed to the formation of the existing Danxia landform.

The Danxia Mountain not only has a beautiful, splendid color, but boasts many unusually shaped stones, the most famous of which are the Male Symbol Stone, Female Symbol Stone and Dragon Scale Stone. The Male Symbol Stone is a huge, standing stone with a height of 28 meters and a diameter of 7 meters, which closely resembles the male organ. The Female Symbol Stone is a long crack on the cliff caused by water erosion, which looks like the male organ's counterpart and is thus called the "mother stone" or the "origin of life." The Male Symbol Stone and the Female Symbol Stone stand opposite each other, as if their co-existence had been carefully arranged by Mother Nature. The Dragon Scale Stone's surface is dotted with several thousand small holes in the shape of beehives, which look like dragon scales. Moss grows abundantly on the stone, and the colors of the moss change with the weather, giving the stone a striking image, like a dragon climbing up the cliff.

The Danxia Mountain has now been made a world geological park, and has also been named "China's Redstone Park".

The Rongbuk Glacier: A City of Ice and Snow

The Rongbuk serac clusters on Mount Qomolangma

The Rongbuk Glacier has a respectable origin, as it is one of the major glaciers nurtured by Mount Qomolangma, the world's highest peak. On the north slope of Mount Qomolangma at an altitude of 5,300–6,300 meters, two major glaciers, the West Rongbuk Glacier and the Central Rongbuk Glacier, gently embrace the pyramid-shaped Mount Qomolangma. They flow along the slope and merge to a length exceeding more than 20 km. The ice layer of the Rongbuk Glacier is more than 300 meters thick at its widest point, while the average width of the glacier tongue reaches over 1,400 meters, making the glacier the largest in the Mount Qomolangma Nature Reserve.

The Rongbuk Glacier boasts the most magnificent serac (masses of ice) clusters in China. At the end of the glacier arrays of seracs can be seen; they stretch for several km and form a wonderful world of ice and snow. The seracs are white, cone-shaped ice columns, which usually stand on gravel-covered mountain slopes and cover a large area. These seracs are crystal-clear and extremely huge, dwarfing any person nearby.

White is not the only color. Under the white coat, each serac displays a pure, light blue, because the ice inside a glacier is constantly under enormous pressure, causing structural changes of ice crystals, as well as changes of the ice's reflection and refraction. The special light blue has become a major feature of glacier ice.

The serac clusters are a rare, natural spectacle, which only exist in continental glaciers at middle and low latitudes. It is impossible for those oceanic glaciers to form serac clusters, as they move too quickly and the glacier tongue at the end melts too rapidly. The continental glaciers in high-latitude regions also have

The beautiful ice columns in the serac clusters

great difficulty in forming any serac clusters, because their glacier tongues only melt a bit. The Rongbuk Glacier happens to have the ideal conditions for forming serac clusters. The ice at the end of the glacier first melts to create cracks, which gradually expands to break the large glacier block into separate ice columns. The ice columns, under the effect of strong winds and sunshine, finally become seracs of various sizes and shapes.

The beautiful serac clusters are also capable of recording history: as the glacier keeps moving, the ice inside is actually snow from many years ago, from which the scientists could glean information about the atmosphere from ancient times. The light-blue serac clusters may be speechless, but they carry the secrets of remote antiquity that are waiting to be decoded one day.

The Hailuogou Glacier: Grand Ice Fall From Heaven

The Hailuogou Glacier maintains several records: it is one of the few glaciers in the world with the steepest fall. It has the most magnificent ice fall in China, and boasts the lowest altitude for the glacier edge among all glaciers at the same latitude in the world. It is also the most avalanche-prone glacier in China, as well as the closest glacier to a Chinese city. What's more important, it also ranks among the most beautiful glaciers in the country.

Hailuogou is located in the Tibetan Autonomous Prefecture of Garze in west Sichuan Province, where more than 70 glaciers in Hailuogou can be found, the most famous of which is the "No.1 Glacier," popularly known as "Grand Ice Fall."

The Grand Ice Fall glacier originates from the eastern highest peak of Gongga Mountain, a famous snowy mountain in Sichuan Province. Along the steep mountain valley, it flows rapidly to an altitude of 3,720 meters,

Hailuogou boasts comparatively low-altitude glaciers which are rare in the world.

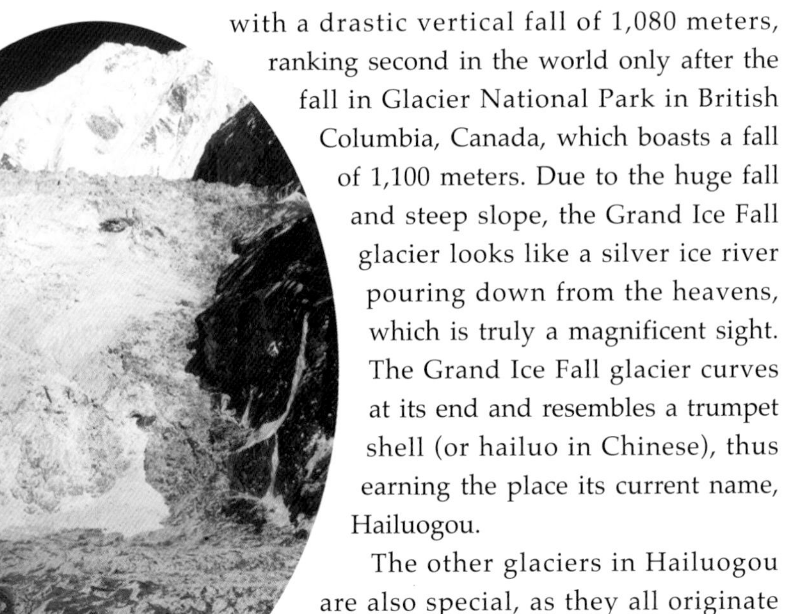

with a drastic vertical fall of 1,080 meters, ranking second in the world only after the fall in Glacier National Park in British Columbia, Canada, which boasts a fall of 1,100 meters. Due to the huge fall and steep slope, the Grand Ice Fall glacier looks like a silver ice river pouring down from the heavens, which is truly a magnificent sight. The Grand Ice Fall glacier curves at its end and resembles a trumpet shell (or hailuo in Chinese), thus earning the place its current name, Hailuogou.

The other glaciers in Hailuogou are also special, as they all originate from the tall, snowy mountains and stretch to places with low altitudes. Some of the glaciers reach altitudes as low as 2,800 meters and even intrude into the forest zone. The combination of dark virgin forests and white, glittering glaciers forms an amazing landscape.

The Grand Ice Fall at Hailuogou looks like a silver ice river pouring down from the heaven.

Situated at a low latitude, the glaciers in Hailuogou move rapidly and are "active." In spring and summer, several hundred glacier avalanches occur in Hailuogou in a single day. When a glacier avalanche occurs, an enormous ice block of more than one million cubic meters collapses suddenly, causing an immense impact that shatters the ice into millions of pieces, as well as thunderously resonating in the mountain valley. The snow fog rising from the avalanche can darken the sky in seconds.

Another amazing spectacle in Hailuogou is that in the vicinity of this wonderland of ice and snow are hot springs with a temperature between 53 and 80 degrees Celsius. The springs gush to form a hot waterfall, and it is special to see the virgin forests clouded in a mixture of the white steam rising from the hot springs and the white snow fog caused by glacier avalanches.

Rivers and Lakes

The Yangtze River: China's Artery

The Yangtze River, China's longest, sets off from the Qinghai-Tibet Plateau, which is reputed to be the "roof of the world," and runs all the way through numerous mountains and valleys to the east until it flows into the Pacific Ocean.

With a total length of more than 6,300 km, the Yangtze is also the world's third longest river, after the Nile in Africa and the Amazon in South America, respectively. The main stream of the Yangtze flows through 11 provinces, autonomous regions and municipalities in China, namely Qinghai, Tibet, Sichuan, Yunnan, Chongqing, Hubei, Hunan, Jiangxi, Anhui, Jiangsu and Shanghai, making the Yangtze one of the most important rivers in the country with the fame of "China's artery."

From west to east, the Yangtze River absorbs several hundred tributaries. The entire Yangtze River water system is like an enormous net that covers a vast region in central China, as well as eight other provinces and autonomous regions, including Guizhou, Gansu, Shaanxi, Henan, Guangxi, Guangdong, Zhejiang and Fujian. The

The origin of the Yangtze River—the Geladaindong Snow Mountain, which is the highest peak in the Dangla Mountains

The first gorge on the Yangtze River—the Tiger-Leaping Gorge. With several huge rocks erecting in the middle of the river, this section of the Yangtze is famous for rushing water and rapid torrents. It was said that the gorge got its current name after a tiger jumped over the river using the huge rocks as its stepping stones.

whole Yangtze River Basin covers 1.8 million sq. km, or one-fifth of China's land territory.

The tributaries provide plenty of water for the Yangtze River, which boasts a total water resource of more than 960 billion cubic meters, or a little more than one-third of the total water resources in all Chinese rivers. The Yangtze River's water resource ranks third in the world, only after the Amazon and the Congo in Africa.

The Yangtze River originates in Qinghai Province, or, more specifically, in the glaciers on the southwest part of Geladaindong Mountain, the highest peak in the Dangla Mountains. The headwaters region boasts high terrains and snow-capped mountains, while snow water from several melting glaciers accumulates drop by drop to give the first water to the Yangtze River.

The upstream of the Yangtze River mainly runs through the mountainous regions with many valleys, featuring swift currents and rushing water. The river first winds through the vast Qinghai-Tibet Plateau, crossing the barren, uninhabited land, and then turns south along the Hengduan Mountains to enter a region full of high

The Jinsha River, an upstream section of the Yangtze River

mountains and deep valleys. At Shigu of Lijiang, Yunnan Province, the river takes a sudden and sharp turn to the northeast, forming the "First Bend of the Yangtze." The river continues to zigzag east and crosses the picturesque Three Gorges to reach Yichang of Hubei Province. The rapid torrents and rushing waters in the upper reaches help the river to store enormous energy, making possible the construction of many water conservancy and hydropower facilities in this river section.

Having passed Yichang, the Yangtze River flows into a vast plain region, known as the Yangtze Plain. The middle and downstream parts of the Yangtze boast the best navigational conditions. The river receives many tributaries in this section and is connected with numerous large and small lakes, as most of China's fresh water lakes lie in this region.

The downstream part of the Yangtze includes the section between Hukou of Jiangxi Province and the mouth of the Yangtze River. In this section, the river course becomes increasingly broader and the river flows more slowly, while shoals of a large or small size can be spotted in the river course occasionally. When the Yangtze finally reaches its destination, the Chongming Island of Shanghai Municipality, its breadth has increased to more than 90 km from the original 1,000-plus meters. This means that a person standing on one bank of the river cannot see across to the other bank.

From the frigid Qinghai-Tibet Plateau to the most prosperous metropolis in China, the Yangtze River has experienced so much. This may explain why the river has become so broad and inclusive when it finally flows into the East China Sea.

The Yellow River: Cradle of the Chinese Civilization

Like a yellow dragon, the Yellow River has written a conspicuous letter "n" on the map of north China before it runs into the Bohai Bay. On its way to the sea, the river has raised the ancestors of the Chinese nation and nurtured one of the world's most ancient civilizations, the Yellow River Civilization.

With a total length of 5,464 km, the Yellow River is the second longest river in China only after the Yangtze River, as well as the fifth longest in the world. It flows through nine provinces and autonomous regions of China, namely Qinghai, Sichuan, Gansu, Ningxia, Inner Mongolia, Shaanxi, Shanxi, Henan and Shandong.

The Yellow River originates in the hinterlands of the Qinghai-Tibet Plateau, with its exact origin at the base of the north slope of the Bayankala Mountains in Qinghai Province. The Bayankala Mountains consist of a host of snowy mountains, and the basin surrounded by the mountains is rich in fountains and lakes, thanks to the melting snow. Two pure fountain streams, namely the Yoigilangleb River and the Kar River, have been confirmed as the authentic origin of the Yellow River. The two small rivers converge with several other streams before flowing into the "Star Sea," a vast swamp comprising numerous water ponds and tiny lakes. Just like a "gas station," the "Star Sea" supplies plenty of water to the Yellow River, turning it into a large river from a narrow stream. After getting more water from two large lakes, namely the Gyaring Lake and the Ngoring Lake, the Yellow River gradually takes on the appearance of a great river.

The water in the upstream section of the Yellow River is pure and clear. The river gets its current name because it flows through the loess plateau, one of the most special landforms in China, in its middle section. The loess plateau is formed through the deposit of wind-blown silt or clay, which pile up to a thickness of tens or even hundreds of kilometers. Cutting through the thick loess layers to form deep valleys in the region, the Yellow River itself also turns yellow after flowing across the plateau. Each year the Yellow River carries away as much as 1.6 billion tons of silt from this region. According to one calculation, if the silt and clay were made into clay blocks each the size of one cubic meter, and if these blocks were lined up along the equator, they could circle the earth more than 20 times.

The silt received in the middle reaches sediment state in the downstream section of the Yellow River, elevating the riverbed year by year. To avoid flooding and possible breaches, the Chinese people over the past 2,000 years have kept constructing and raising the Yellow River levees, while the excessive sediment deposits have continuously raised the riverbed until it is now more than 10 meters over the surrounding grounds. This unique spectacle is called "hanging river" or "suspended river." Despite the

The Yellow River winds through the Zoige Grassland of Sichuan Province.

The natural landscape of the Loess Plateau, featuring tens of thousands of ravines and gullies. The serious soil erosion of the Loess Plateau has made the Yellow River the world's most silt-ridden river.

sediment deposits, the majority of the silt carried by the Yellow River reaches the mouth of the river in Dongying City of Shandong Province, creating new land. The land is dramatically described as "a land created by an earth-spitting dragon." It is expected that, sooner or later, the Bohai Bay of China will be filled by the silt of the Yellow River.

The Yellow River is seen as the "mother river of the Chinese nation" and a "cradle of Chinese civilization." Ever since the Neolithic Age (c. 10,000 years ago–4,000 years ago), the Yellow River Basin has played a leading role in the development of the Chinese civilization and culture. The Yellow River Civilization was initiated by such legendary ancestors of the Chinese nation as Suirenshi, Fuyi and Shennong. The Shang (1600–1046 BC) and Zhou (1046–256 BC) dynasties were based in the Yellow River Basin, which date back more than 3,000 years ago, marking the origin of China's written history. Later, a

The Hukou Waterfall in the middle reaches of the Yellow River

succession of Chinese feudal dynasties, including Qin (221–206 BC), the Western Han (206 BC–AD 25), the Eastern Han (25–220), Wei (220–265), the Western Jin(265–316), Sui (581–618), Tang and the Northern Song (960–1127), all established their capital cities in the Yellow River Basin. For a long, historical period, the Yellow River Basin had served as China's political, economic and cultural center.

The Yellow River also boasts a lot of magnificent and beautiful scenic spots, the most famed of which is the Hukou Waterfall located in the Shanxi-Shaanxi Yellow River Valley in the middle reaches. Lying in Jixian County of Shanxi Province, the Hukou Waterfall witnesses a sudden narrowing of the Yellow River riverbed, where the roaring yellow waters make a steep fall of some 30 meters as if poured out from a gigantic pot.

The Three Gorges: Beyond Time and Space

The Three Gorges boast the most magnificent landscape on the Yangtze River, China's longest. For thousands of years, numerous poems have been written to highlight the beauty of the Three Gorges. As a symbol of China's natural landscape, the Three Gorges area was selected as the main theme on Chinese banknotes several times.

The Three Gorges section of the Yangtze River starts from Baidicheng, an ancient city at the base of the Bashan Mountain in Chongqing Municipality, on the west, and ends at Nanjin Pass of Yichang City, Hubei Province on the east, with a total length of 192 km. It is mainly composed of three gorge sections, namely the Qutang Gorge, Wuxia Gorge and Xiling Gorge.

The Qutang Gorge, also called the Kuixia Gorge, is the beginning section of the Three Gorges. It is 8 km long, stretching from Baidicheng on the west to Daxi

Town of Wushan County on the east. It is the shortest yet most magnificent section of the Three Gorges. At both the entrance and exit of the Qutang Gorge stand high, steep mountains with a height of 1,000 to 1,500 meters. The mountains on both sides of the river look just like a gate, while the narrowest section of the river course only has a breadth of less than 100 meters, where the currents run wildly and rapidly. The Qutang Gorge area boasts a concentration of famous historical sites and precious cultural relics, including the ancient cities of Fengjie and Baidicheng, the rocky Eight Battle Formation, the temple of ancient general Zhang Fei at Yunyang, the ancient plank road built along the cliffs, the King Fisher's Cave, and the relics of the ancient Daxi Civilization.

Following the Qutang Gorge is the Wuxia Gorge, which is famous for its beautiful scenery. The Wuxia Gorge is 46 km long and extends from the Daning River mouth near the county seat of Wushan County on the west to Guandukou of Badong County, Hubei Province on the east. The Wuxia Gorge area features deep valleys and long, twisted ravines, with unusually shaped peaks

The Qutang Gorge

The Wuxia Gorge

standing high on both sides. The renowned "12 Peaks of the Wushan Mountain" have appealed to poets of all generations with their distinct characteristics and natural charm. Due to the depth and length of the ravines, the region has a humid environment and the peaks are often shrouded in cloud and mist. Thus, an ancient poem says, "One who has seen the ocean will not be interested in seeing other waters, and one who has visited the Wushan Mountain will not be interested in seeing clouds anywhere else." There are also many historical sites and relics in the Wuxia Gorge area, such as the ancient plank road built along the cliffs, and the countless marks of towlines left on the riverside rocks by the toiling boat-trackers.

The almost-70 km Xiling Gorge is the last section of the Three Gorges, and it lies between Xiangxikou of Zigui County in Yichang City of Hubei Province and Nanjin

The Xiling Gorge

Pass of Yichang. The section is famous for its complicated terrain, dangerous shoals and rushing waters. The Xiling Gorge features a mixture of large and small ravines and dangerous shoals, and the Yangtze River roars through this section with many currents. The Xiling Gorge used to be the most dangerous section for shipping on the Yangtze, but thanks to the continuous efforts since the ancient times to clear the waterway and remove the hidden reefs, navigational safety in this section can now be guaranteed.

The Xiling Gorge is also where the construction of the Three Gorges Water Conservancy and Hydropower Project (also called the Three Gorges Project, in short) is underway. The gigantic project, which is the largest of its kind in the world, involves the construction of a 3,035-meter-long, 185-meter-high dam, a hydroelectricity plant and navigational facilities. Once completed, the Three Gorges Project will add a new, magnificent landscape to the Three Gorges scenery.

The Three Gorges region is both beautiful and rich in historical and cultural heritage. Having left indelible marks on the Chinese culture in ancient times, it remains an important region for the Chinese economy and culture today.

The Three Parallel Rivers: Dancing Mountains and Rivers

The region of the Three Parallel Rivers is a singular geographical wonder in the world. As shown in satellite photos, three great rivers, which are separated by four majestic mountains, flow parallel within a narrow belt for scores of kilometers.

Instead of one scenic spot, the Three Parallel Rivers actually refer to a vast region in northwest Yunnan Province. In this region, three major rivers originating from the Qinghai-Tibet Plateau, namely the Jinsha River, Lancang River and Nujiang River, flow parallel from north to south for 170 km without converging, and form a rare geographical landscape. All three rivers enjoy great fame: the Jinsha River is actually upstream of China's longest river, the Yangtze. The Lancang River becomes the most important river in Southeast Asia, the Mekong, after flowing out of China in the south. The Nujiang River, after leaving China, is called the Salween River, a major river in Myanmar and Thailand.

Located at the convergence of the three geographical regions of East Asia, South Asia and the Qinghai-Tibet Plateau, the region of the Three Parallel Rivers is a typical model of the formation and evolution of the mountain landform on earth. Some 40 million years ago, the Indian Subcontinental Plate and the Eurasian Plate had a major collision, which caused the steep rise of the Hengduan Mountains and led to the existing landform in the Three Parallel Rivers region.

The Three Parallel Rivers region boasts high mountains and deep valleys, with a sharp difference in elevation. There are great snowy mountains in this region, including the sacred mountain for the Tibetans, the Meili Snow Mountain, whose highest peak Kawagabo has an elevation of 6,740 meters. There are also river valleys of low altitudes, like the Nujiang River Valley, with an elevation of only 700 meters, where the weather

The Lancang River Grand Canyon in Deqin County of Yunnan Province features steep mountains, deep valleys, rushing water and dense forest.

The Nujiang River takes a sharp turn at Bingzhongluo Town, Gongshan County of Yunnan Province, forming a half-circle bend popularly called "the first bend of the Nujiang River." A flat and broad mini-plain in the shape of a peninsula facing water on three sides exists in the area.

The Yunnan snub-nosed monkey. It is a primate only found in China, which mainly lives in the Three Parallel Rivers region of Yunnan. The animal looks charming and cute with erecting black hairs on the top of its head, apricot-shaped eyes, a rising nose and thick, red lips.

is so dry and hot that raindrops evaporate before they reach the ground. The huge elevational differences have made it possible for a variety of natural landscapes to co-exist in the region of the Three Parallel Rivers, such as snowy mountains, glaciers, meadows, lakes, plateau wetlands, coniferous forests, broad-leaf forests, and dry and hot river valleys.

Thanks to its special geological structure, the Three

Parallel Rivers area also becomes one of the few regions in the world with the richest biological species. The region only accounts for less than 0.4 percent of China's land territory, but is home to more than 20 percent of the higher plants and over 25 percent of the animal species so far found in the country. As this region was free from the coverage of continental glaciers in the Quaternary Ice Age, and the mountains in this region all have a north-south orientation, the region has served as a main north-south migratory channel and a refuge for animal species on the Eurasian Continent. Many species have survived climatic changes on the earth in this region, while their peers in other places have fallen victim to such changes. Among the survivors are more than 70 animal species under China's state protection, such as the Yunnan snub-nosed monkey, antelope, snow leopard, Bengal tiger and black-necked crane, as well as over 30 plants under state protection including Taiwania flousiana, spinulose tree ferns, and taxus chinensis.

Firs and rhododendron bushes in the Qianhushan Scenic Area of the Three Parallel Rivers region. The Qianhushan Scenic Area boasts a complete and unique alpine eco-system, mainly featuring the alpine meadow, fir forest and rhododendron bushes.

The Kanas Lake: Unparalleled Beauty

The Kanas Lake is hidden deeply at the base of the Friendship Peak of the Altai Mountain in Xinjiang. On a map of China, which shows the country in the shape of a rooster, the lake is located at the tip of the rooster's tail. Most people will be overwhelmed by the lake's beauty at first sight.

The Kanas Lake used to be part of the Kanas River. Later, as a result of glacier movements, the river course was blocked and the lake came into being. The lake is surrounded by high mountains, whose tops are coated by snow but slopes are covered by dense forests and colorful wild flowers.

The water in the Kanas Lake presents a spectrum of colors along with the changing weather and seasons. Sometimes it is pure blue or emerald green, and other times turquoise blue or white and gray. On some occasions the lake even shows a mixture of multiple colors at the same time. Therefore, the lake is reputed as a "color-changing lake."

The lake looks more charming and mysterious at dawn and dusk.

Before daybreak, the lake reflects light clouds in the sky, while the surrounding mountains are all shrouded in mist and cannot be seen at all. The silver-white surface of the lake is extremely peaceful without the slightest ripple. The Kanas Lake at this moment is still "in a sound sleep." Sometimes a couple of early-rising birds fly across the lake, their shadows reflecting in the water so clearly that it looks as though four birds are flying together.

The landscape of the lake at dusk is quite different from that in the early morning. Even in a mid-summer month like June, the night temperature here will drop below 10 degrees Celsius. Light snow starts to fall, but only on the mountainside, never falling into the lake. People by the lake can see clearly the whole process of a forest turning white amidst the light snow. When

The Kanas Lake used to be the broadest part of the Kanas River.

evening falls, the surface of the lake gradually turns dark blue, while a light fog slowly rises above the lake and gradually merges into the shades of the night.

The Kanas Lake enjoys the fame of "color-changing lake," always presenting a spectrum of colors such as emerald green, white and gray, pink and turquoise blue.

Besides the extremely beautiful scenery, the Kanas Lake boasts another major attraction, the legendary "lake monster." The story of the "lake monster" can be traced back to long ago, as some people claimed that they had accidentally seen a strange animal reveal its head from the water at dusk or daybreak. Judging from the scale of the splashes of the water, the people claimed that this animal had a gigantic body—probably 10 meters long. The local herdsmen also provided additional evidence about the existence of the "lake monster." They claimed that some oxen and horses went missing while drinking from the lake, and afterwards they could only find random hoofprints of the animals by the lake. They also ruled out the possibility of the animals slipping down and falling into the lake themselves, as the ground on the lakeside was solid.

Over the past years several teams of explorers have come to the lake in an attempt to reveal the truth about the "lake monster." They dove into the lake, set up traps or lay baits, but all efforts ended in vain. However, they did find a huge predatory fish—the giant red fish—in the lake, and suspected that it might be the alleged "lake monster." With the official name of *taimen*, the giant red

fish shows a red-brown color in its breeding season and is aggressive by nature. Some people believe that there might be some extremely large *taimen* living in the Kanas Lake, which have a body length of more than 10 meters and therefore are large and strong enough to drag away and swallow down oxen and horses, thus triggering the tales of the legendary "lake monster."

The Sleeping Dragon Bay—a famous scenic spot at the Kanas Lake. It is a small isle in the middle of the river bay, which looks like a dragon lying still in the water while observed from high places.

The Namco Lake: Heavenly Lake on the Plateau

In the Tibetan language, *nam* means "heaven" and *co* means "lake," so the literal meaning of Namco is "the lake of heaven." This name suits the lake well, as it is very close to the sky: with an elevation of 4,718 meters, the Namco Lake is the highest salt water lake in the world. The lake is also as broad as the sky, with a length of 70 km and a width of 30 km, covering nearly 2,000 sq. km and ranking second in size among all salt water lakes in China. The lake is also as blue as the sky, with its wide, open surface reflecting the blue sky and white clouds. The lake is as holy as the heaven in Tibetan Buddhism, ranking among the three sacred lakes in the Tibetan region.

The Namco Lake is located on the vast northern Tibet grassland, with the snow-capped Nyainqentanglha Mountain Range stretching along it just like an enormous dyke guarding the sacred lake. According to local folk tales, the Nyainqentanglha Mountain Range and the Namco Lake are a loving couple who help each other to survive the frigid environment on the plateau.

In reality, the Nyainqentanglha Mountain Range acts as the Namco Lake's assistant, as melting snow from the mountains supplies water to the lake. The water in the Namco Lake is extremely pure and clear, because the lake has a very clean and pure origin. When heavy winds blow across the north Tibet grasslands, blue and green waves also surge in the Namco Lake, like large pieces of emerald in various shapes.

The Namco Lake has a natural gate, which is composed of two huge rocks standing on the lakeside. With a dark yellow, the rocks are actually two separate, independent stone columns standing opposite each other. With a height of more than 30 meters each, the two columns stand eight meters from each other, and the road to the lake just passes between them. Viewing them as

Namco, a place that combines the beauty of snow mountain and highland lake.

the "doormen" of the Namco Lake, people call the stone columns "a divine gate."

After passing the "divine gate," many traces of lake worship can be seen; these were left over by pilgrims of the Tibetan Buddhism. At the end of the 12th century, the

most revered monks of the Tibetan Buddhism arrived at the Namco Lake for self-cultivation, and they established the sacred religious status of the lake. Since then, believers of the Tibetan Buddhism have never ceased paying pilgrimage to and worshipping the Namco Lake. On the lakeside are a large array of scripture streamers that occupy several hundred sq. meters, with strings of colorful flags fluttering in the wind. The scripture streamer is a string of small flags, each with Tibetan Buddhist scriptures. It is believed that when the flag flutters once in the wind, the scriptures on it are recited once on behalf of the person who put it up.

There are also large and small Mani piles by the lake. The Mani piles are actually piles of stones, some of which are natural and others have beautiful images of Buddha or scriptures carved on them. Believers of the Tibetan Buddhism think that the Mani piles are supernatural. On every festival or religious holiday, they add stones to the

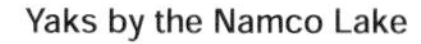

Yaks by the Namco Lake

Mani piles by the Namco Lake

Mani piles while chanting Buddhist scriptures, and hold rituals to worship Buddha by the piles. Year after year the Mani piles have grown large and tall, with every stone in the pile carrying the sincere wishes and pious prayers of the believers. Many carvings on the Mani stones are also great artistic works.

The grandest ritual of worship at the Namco Lake takes place every Year of the Goat on the Tibetan calendar. The legends say that goat is the zodiac sign of the Namco Lake, and that one gains enormous comfort and happiness by circling around the lake in the Year of the Goat. So, when the Tibetan Year of the Goat arrives once every 12 years, tens of thousands of Buddhists flock to the region and circle around the lake on foot. It takes four or five days for them to complete a circle, and they devotedly pray to Buddha with every step they take.

The Qinghai Lake: A Sea in the Heart of the Land

Located in northeast Qinghai-Tibet Plateau, the Qinghai Lake is the largest inland salt water lake in China. It is so broad and expansive that the ancient people mistook it for a sea.

The Qinghai Lake adds a gentle touch to the rough plateau. It is surrounded by four tall mountains, each with an elevation between 3,000 and 4,000 meters, which embrace the lake like natural shields. From the lakeside to the foot of the mountains lie vast, flat grasslands that stretches for several hundred km. The magnificent mountains, serene lake and elegant grassland form a

A satellite picture of the Qinghai Lake

charming landscape.

New visitors to the Qinghai Lake are often surprised to see that the water in the lake is not a single color: the lake presents a spectrum of hues, such as sky blue, emerald green, dark purple and silver gray in correspondence with the changing weather. The sight of the mist-covered lake surface and the glittering waves can dissolve fatigue and worries.

Due to its gentle nature, the Qinghai Lake is linked with stories about women. In Chinese mythology, the Qinghai Lake is also called the "Pond of Fairy Mother's Abode," whose owner is a prestigious goddess, the Queen Mother of the Western Heaven. It is said that the Queen Mother held grand banquets in the pond to entertain other gods and goddesses in the heaven. As the Queen Mother's birthday was said to be July 18 on the Chinese lunar calendar, both officials and ordinary people would come to the lakeside to hold grand rituals of worship on this day, which has become a regular practice ever since the Tang Dynasty. Today, the lake worshipping ceremony has evolved into a grand party. People from all over gather by the lake—singing, dancing, playing games and holding competitions to have fun and make friends.

A small island, Haixinshan (which literally means "a mountain in the heart of the sea"), can be found in the lake, and many legendary stories revolve around it. Haixinshan is 30 km from the south lakeshore, and is a long, narrow island 2.3 km long and 0.8 km wide. The rocky island boasts freshwater springs that attract birds. The ancient Chinese believed that the island was the only place to breed the precious "dragon horses." It is said that in winter when the Qinghai Lake froze, the local herdsmen would drive the mares onto the Haixinshan Island, where they could become impregnated with the "dragon's offspring." Thus, the colts they bore would grow into "dragon horses," being not only tall and striking but strong and fast, making them ideal battle horses. People today believe that the "dragon horses" actually refer to a fine breed named "*Qinghaicong*," which

The Qinghai Lake is a paradise for birds, which hover in the sky freely and add much vitality to the tranquil lake.

can only be found near the Qinghai Lake.

However, the most charming part of the Qinghai Lake is the birds' islands, which are located in the northwest. There are two such islands, namely, the Dandao Island (island of the eggs) and Haixipi Island. Both accommodate a large number of migratory birds and thus have the reputation as a "Kingdom of the Birds."

Covering about 1 sq. km, the Dandao Island is not large but attracts numerous birds. Each year, more than 100,000 migratory birds arrive at the island for inhabiting or breeding. When spring arrives, the island is occupied by a variety of migratory birds, such as the bar-headed goose, brown-headed gull and great black-headed gull, whose nests can be spotted everywhere. It has become a marvelous spectacle of the Qinghai Lake that the whole island is densely covered by eggs laid by the migratory birds settling down.

The size of the Haixipi Island is four times larger than that of the Dandao Island. The most special aspect of the

island is that it houses an "empire of cormorants." On a huge rock standing in east Haixipi Island, which looks just like a giant bell turned upside down, a large army of black cormorants can be found. With binoculars, the cormorants can be seen taking a comfortable sunbath and leading free, easy lives.

The erecting huge rock on the "cormorant island" has almost become a symbol of the Birds' Islands in the Qinghai Lake.

Now, a nature reserve has been established in the Qinghai Lake, to better protect the birds and also the environment. The beautiful legends of the lake will surely last forever.

Jiuzhaigou: A Colorful Painting

Jiuzhaigou (which literally means "valley of nine villages) boasts a concentration of alpine lakes, and the lakes, streams and waterfalls in this area are extraordinarily colorful, as if Mother Nature drew a wonderful painting here.

In mountainous north Sichuan Province, Jiuzhaigou covers more than 700 sq. km. It is a Y-shaped mountain valley, consisting of one main ravine and two branch ravines, and received its name because there are nine Tibetan villages in the valley. Sandwiched by high

The Nuorilang Waterfall, a unique spectacle of water flowing through a dense forest

mountains, Jiuzhaigou has preserved a primitive appearance with dense virgin forests and more than 100 large and small lakes are scattered in the long, narrow valley, which are interconnected by numerous streams and waterfalls, forming a unique water landscape.

Entering Jiuzhaigou along the main ravine, the serene and peaceful Rhinoceros Lake is reached first. The lake's broad, calm surface and pure, blue water help to purify the heart and soul, and stir great imagination.

Further upstream the two branch ravines is the

heartland of the great mountains. The branch ravine on the right leads to the thunderous Nuorilang Waterfall. Though not steep, the Nuorilang Waterfall is the widest waterfall in China, with a breadth of 320 meters.

Winding through the Nuorilang Waterfall, the stream in the ravine suddenly turns extremely wide while the water becomes shallow. The water currents are blocked by many stones and fallen tree branches, splashing in all directions and glittering like rolling pearls in the sunshine. The special scene has gained this place a striking name, the "Pearl Beach."

Deeper in the mountains are a series of colorful, splendid lakes, with beautiful names such as "Five-Flower Lake," "Panda Lake" and "Swan Lake." The water in these lakes boasts a wide range of colors—from sapphire blue and emerald green to turquoise blue and light purple. The reflections of the blue sky, white clouds,

The Five-Flower Lake, reputed as "the soul of Jiuzhaigou". The lake is rich in calcium carbonate and water plants and therefore can present splendid colors in the sunshine. In autumn, the colors of the leaves in the forest are changing, reflecting all kinds of tints—yellow, red, green and white, to name a few—to the lake. The color variety extends far beyond the imagination of any painter.

Many "tree sculptures" can be spotted soaking in the crystal clear, light blue stream.

snowy mountains, and colorful trees and flowers on the calm lake surface lends even more colors to these lakes. This place is most beautiful in autumn, when the colors of the leaves in the forest are changing, reflecting all kinds of tints—yellow, red, green and white, to name a few—to the lake. It's truly a "painting masterpiece," whose color variety extends far beyond the imagination of any painter.

The branch ravine on the left is equally appealing in terms of the natural landscape. The bright Five-Color Lake and the mountain-embraced Long Lake both carry the charming reflections of the snowy mountains and forests around them. The most special scene lies under the water, as many "tree sculptures" can be spotted, soaking in the light blue stream. These are just common pine trees commonly seen on the stream banks, but the trunks of the "tree sculptures" look thicker and smoother than the original ones. The secret lies with the content of the water, which is rich in calcium carbonate due to the limestone at Jiuzhaigou. The decayed trunks of the dead pine trees, after falling into the stream, are gradually coated by calcium in the water and turn into these natural sculptures.

Deserts and Grasslands

The Taklimakan Desert: Graveyard of Ancient Civilizations

The Taklimakan Desert is the largest desert in China, as well as the second largest mobile desert in the world. With a total area of 330,000 sq. km, the desert is as vast as the sea, stretching for more than 1,000 km from east to west and over 400 km from north to south. The boundless sea of sand in the desert has

The heartland of the Taklimakan Desert is dominated by a boundless sea of sand.

won it the fame as a "sea of death," which "one can enter but will never leave." However, in the Uygur language, "taklimakan" means "the old homeland," because in ancient times the place was not a desert, but a beautiful oasis that had nurtured numerous brilliant civilizations.

Located in the center of the Tarim Basin in China's Xinjiang Uygur Autonomous Region, the Taklimakan Desert lies in the hinterland of the Eurasian Continent, surrounded on three sides by mountains more than 4,000 meters above sea level: the Tianshan Mountains in the north, the Qinghai-Tibet Plateau in the south, and the Pamirs in the west. Rainfall is extremely rare in this region, which only has scorching sun, freezing nights and ceaseless gales.

Nevertheless, the region is not a forbidden zone for life. The surrounding high mountains, while blocking the entry of humid air, also supply pure water with their melting snow. The Hotan River, Keriya River, Niya River and Andir River—all originated from the snowy mountains and flowed across the desert. Some of them dispersed in the heartland of the desert, while others nurtured "green corridors" on the yellow sand one after another. Thanks to the existence of these great rivers, the Silk Road emerged from a "sea of death" and the desert became a land of prosperity that witnessed the exchange between several major civilizations.

Seeds in the desert

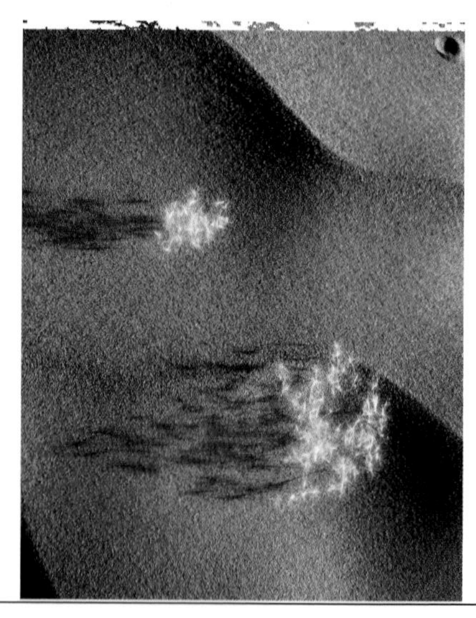

The Silk Road appeared in historical records in as early as the 1st century BC during China's Han Dynasty. With a total length of more than 70,000 km, the road crossed Central Asia to link the ancient Chinese civilization with other civilizations created by the ancient Greeks, Egyptians, Babylonians and Indians. In the following centuries, these great civilizations converged in the Taklimakan Desert, proved today by the excavation of a large quantity of precious, world-stunning

Some prosperous ancient cities are now buried beneath the endless dunes of the Taklimakan Desert.

cultural relics. The relics include portraits of winged angels, brocades from China, Roman-style columns, and statues of Buddha from India. Via the Silk Road, Chinese technologies and inventions such as silkworm breeding, gunpowder and papermaking were introduced to Central Asia and even Rome, while Jing Jiao (or Illustrious Religion), Islam, astronomy and mathematics also spread to China from the West. The Silk Road had changed the history of the world, and the Taklimakan Desert has borne witness to such significant changes.

According to the ancient history records of China, there used to be 36 kingdoms in the so-called "Western Frontier Regions," all enjoying great prosperity and they scattered in the Taklimakan Desert like pearls. However, due to climate changes over the past several thousand years, the desert has gradually shown its cruel side, swallowing one oasis after another mercilessly and burying all those prosperous kingdoms under endless dunes.

Starting from the 19th century, the Taklimakan Desert has become a paradise and treasure house for explorers and archaeologists all over the world. Loulan, Niya, and Miran, those ancient city states that used to live only in history books have been discovered and excavated one after another. Nevertheless, the boundless Taklimakan Desert is still keeping too many secrets to itself, and there remain too many unsolved riddles of history and civilization.

The Badain Jaran Desert: On Top of All Deserts

The Badain Jaran Desert is famous for its grand, magnificent dunes. The highest sand hill in the desert boasts a relative height of more than 500 meters—the world record so far—and is thus reputed as the "Mount Qomolangma in the desert."

Located in the Alxa League in west China's Inner Mongolia Autonomous Region, the Badain Jaran Desert has a total area of 47,000 sq. km and is the third largest desert in China and fourth largest in the world. In the heartland of the desert, the average height of the sand hills reaches 200 meters. From an aerial view, the endless dunes look like surging waves in a sea, though in gold.

It's no easy job to cross the desert, as there are so many sand hills with many slopes and sand pits. Even camels backslide when they try to tread uphill, and downhill is slippery. On the slopes of the sand hills grow many desert

With a total area of 47,000 sq. km, the Badain Jaran Desert has a magnificent spectacle.

From an aerial view, the endless dunes look like surging waves in a sea, though in gold.

Sand-based plants grow sparsely in the quicksand-ridden Badain Jaran Desert. The photo shows some sand shallots growing in the desert.

plants, which all have thorny, needle-shaped leaves and are yellow-green or gray-white. The desert cicadas hide themselves in the plants, singing ceaselessly, while the yellow-brown desert lizards on the slopes watch vigilantly, ready to run at any sign of potential danger.

The sand rolls and moves whenever the wind blows. Actually, all the magnificent sand hills in the desert have come into being due to the winds. As a result, all these hills share the same features, with one slope being very smooth and the other, very steep, and with the same orientation. The wind here is so ferocious that it can easily blow the sand several hundred meters to the top of a dune. Sometimes a dune becomes too high to sustain

The deep, blue *Haizi* adds beauty and charm to the barren desert.

itself and collapses suddenly, with a roar that pierces throughout the desert.

Despite the arid nature of the desert, some small, blue lakes are hidden in it, which the locals call *Haizi* ("mini-seas"). The Badain Jaran Desert boasts more than 100 such small lakes, each surrounded by a vibrant oasis.

Just imagine how thrilled a lonely traveler would be upon seeing an oasis in the middle of a desert. Most *Haizi* are filled with pure, blue salt water, and the brine shrimps in the water provide sufficient food for numerous wild ducks and other water fowl. There is also an abundance of plants on the lakeside, such as reeds, weeping willows and oleasters. Under these trees, goats graze happily and camels chew cud quietly. In the desert several freshwater springs also exist, which continuously gush out of the sand and offer a cool, sweet drink to thirsty people or livestock.

The Badain Jaran Desert is by no means a barren, lifeless wasteland, but a place full of vitality.

The Hulun Buir Grassland: A Thousand-Year-Old Idyllic Song

"The heaven is unlimited and the earth boundless. The oxen and sheep only appear when the wind brings down the grasses." This ancient Chinese poem can serve as a vivid description of the charming landscape on the Hulun Buir Grassland. On the top of the rooster-shaped Chinese map, there is a place resembling the rooster's comb. That is the Hulun Buir Grassland, one of the most beautiful and prosperous grasslands in China, dubbed "a jade in North China."

Located in northeast Inner Mongolia Autonomous Region, the Hulun Buir Grassland covers more than

Flocks of sheep and oxen roam around on the vast, green grassland of Hulun Buir.

100,000 sq. km, stretching for 300 km from east to west and 200 km from south to north. Under the blue sky dotted with white clouds, the vast grassland features a tranquil yet lively scene: Flowers blossom everywhere in a sea of grass, oxen and sheep chase each other freely, and herdsmen sing while carrying whips. This is the best preserved grassland in China, where more than 100 kinds of pasture crops rich in nutrients, such as wild rye, needlegrass and alfalfa, thrive and carpet the ground. This is also a pure, sacred land, free of pollution—a reason why livestock products such as meat, milk, leather and wool from this region are so popular with people across the country.

Free from pollution and with a comparatively better protected ecological environment, the Hulun Buir Grassland is dotted with twisted rivers and numerous lakes.

There is a beautiful legend about how the grassland got its current name: long ago, many demons inhabited the grassland; they often ravaged pastures and slaughtered livestock. A pair of young lovers of the local Mongolian tribe—a pretty, brave girl named Hulun and

The local people of Hulun Buir sing and dance to celebrate the Naadam festival at the largest get-together venue in the Inner Mongolia Autonomous Region. The once-a-year Naadam, which literally means entertainment and games in Mongolian, is a traditional occasion for the Mongolian people to get together and have fun.

a handsome, strong boy named Buir—fought the demons valiantly and eventually turned themselves into two lakes, drowning all the demons. To date, the Hulun Lake and Buir Lake continue to nurture all lives on the grassland.

Besides the Hulun and Buir Lakes are several hundred other lakes, large and small, scattered on the vast grassland like stars in the sky. There are also more than 3,000 rivers winding through the region, flowing freely without any topographical restriction, thanks to the flat, smooth terrain. The Murgler River, whose course has many more bends and twists than the famous Yellow River, is reputed as "the most twisted river

Horse race, a traditional sports activity for the Mongolians.

in the world."

The Hulun Buir Grassland is also the origin of the Mongolian civilization. The Ergune River Basin on the grassland used to be a main battlefield for the great Mongolian leader Genghis Khan. Today, the Hulun Buir Grassland is still home to the Mongolians, who lead modern lives but prefer to live in the Mongolian tents on the grassland. With cooking smoke rising from the tent chimneys, oxen and sheep grazing at ease and horses galloping around, the Hulun Buir Grassland still presents a charming, idyllic song that has lasted for a thousand years.

Bayanbulak: A Swan Lake in the Embrace of Snowy Mountains

Bayanbulak is a beautiful wetland, surrounded by snow-capped mountains. It accommodates three-fifths of the world's total swan population, living up to the name of "Home of Swans."

In the Mongolian language, Bayanbulak means "fountain of affluence." It is located in central Xinjiang and lies in the heartland of the Tianshan Mountains. With an elevation of 2,300 to 3,100 meters, it enjoys

The Bayanbulak Grassland lies in the heartland of the Tianshan Mountains.

Winding rivers, which look like silver silk ribbons, flow across the grassland.

a mild climate with no distinct seasons. Encircled by snowy mountains, the region boasts 100,000 hectares of fertile grassland nurtured by snow water from melting glaciers. Just as a child being well-nurtured by his mother, Bayanbulak has received plenty of water from the surrounding snowy mountains and has become one of the best wetlands in Xinjiang with a high concentration of rivers and lakes.

The "swan lake" of Bayanbulak is located on the grassland, in southwest Bayan Town. It is actually a large swamp comprising numerous, interconnected small lakes.

As China's first nature reserve for swans, the "swan lake" is truly a paradise for the birds. It is home to tens of thousands of swans of various species, including whooper swan, whistling swan and mute swan. They build their nests in the food-abundant swamp and lead

The Swan Lake in the sunset.
Each spring after snowmelt, tens of thousands of rare and precious birds, mainly whooper swans, whistling swans and mute swans, arrive at the Swan Lake to settle and breed.

an easy, happy life in the lakes. At times of leisure, they either plume their white feathers with their bills or sing loudly and excitedly. The most charming scene on the lake is a group of swans dancing a "water ballet" together. The local residents regard the swans as "birds of purity and chastity" and "a symbol of good luck." Therefore, they have never tried to capture any swans, guaranteeing a safe and peaceful living environment for the birds.

In addition to swans, Bayanbulak also accommodates nearly 130 other birds, such as the black stork, golden eagle, imperial eagle and snow cock. For those long-distance-travelling, exhausted migrating birds, Bayanbulak is a warm, peaceful and safe haven forever.

The beautiful swans

Zoige: A Highland Jade

The largest and best preserved plateau wetland in the world, Zoige lies in east China's Qinghai-Tibet Plateau like a beautiful piece of jade.

With an area greater than 100 hectares and an elevation of 3,400 to 3,600 meters, Zoige lies on the boundary of Sichuan and Gansu Provinces and is a swamp wetland on the Qinghai-Tibet Plateau least affected by human

activity. Travelling along the boundary of Sichuan and Gansu from east to west, a host of high mountain ranges will be encountered first, but hidden behind the mountains is a vast wetland as flat as a carpet—Zoige.

The magnificent Qinghai-Tibet Plateau, dubbed "the roof of the world," reveals its gentle side at Zoige: numerous flowers bloom among the green grass, most of which are light yellow. When the wind blows, the flowers sway back and forth, like yellow waves surging on a

International experts on wetland call Zoige "the world's largest and most original plateau wetland least affected by human activity."

Flowers, lakes, water and grass at Zoige

green sea. The wetland also boasts tranquil lakes and winding rivers, in which the blue sky is reflected. Many people tend to use words like "frigid" and "barren" to describe a plateau, but Zoige is an exception.

In summer, when pasture crops thrive in Zoige, Tibetan herdsmen drive their oxen and sheep here and pitch their black tents in which to live. When they make milk teas, smoke spirals from the tents and dissipates in the air. At Zoige, visitors enjoy the grassland landscape and listen to the herdsmen singing on horseback, and the fortunate ones are invited by the herdsmen to join them in tasting cheese cakes, drinking butter tea and eating a whole roasted sheep.

For the wildlife, Zoige is also a rare highland haven. Water nurtures a highland jade like Zoige, while Zoige nurtures much wildlife. Each summer, the world's only crane that calls the plateau its breeding place—the black-necked crane—arrives at Zoige to settle and breed.

The black-necked crane, a bird species under China's first-class state protection, is the world's only crane that calls the plateau its breeding place.

Accompanying the cranes are herds of wild donkeys and yellow antelope. Featuring a typical eco-system of an alpine wetland, Zoige ranks among the few plateau regions in China with the richest bio-diversity.

What's more important, Zoige also plays a major role in water conservation of the upstream of the Yellow River, China's second longest river, which has nurtured the country's splendid, ancient civilization. Now Zoige has been evaluated as a "key wetland in the world," a name it rightly deserves, not only because of its beauty, but also its significant role as the "kidney of the earth."

The Yellow River Delta Wetland: The Youngest Soil

Usually it takes millions of years for a sea to turn into land, but this could be realized in a few months at the Yellow River Delta. Only here can the rapid transformation of land and sea be witnessed.

The Yellow River Delta is located at the river's estuary in north Shandong Province. Like a huge yellow dragon, the Yellow River carries a large quantity of sand and silt and roars through until it gushes into Bohai Bay, dyeing a large area yellow. Each year the river carries more than one billion tons of sand and silt from the inland to its estuary, which gathers sediment to form the "newest land" on the earth and constantly pushes the coastline forward, at an annual average speed of 2 to 3 km. As a result, China sees an increase of its land by scores of sq. km every year.

The Yellow River Delta is a huge sector of land centered at the course of the Yellow River, with those areas farthest from the sea in existence from the earliest times. Therefore, walking from the inland to the seaside along the river can yield answers to the mystery of the transformation of land and sea.

The areas that came into earliest being are now fertile farmland, and villages of red-bricked, tile-roofed houses have developed amidst the farmland. The closer the soil is to the sea, the younger the soil and the fewer traces of human activity. On a broad field grow numerous reeds, which in autumn look gold, with their white fluffy tips swaying in the wind like surging waves. In the boundless reed marshes lie countless creeks and ponds, which offer a perfect habitat for birds.

The Yellow River Delta happens to sit on the flight route of migratory birds from North Asia, and it has become an "international airport" for the passing birds with its excellent, natural environment. The reed marshes in the Yellow River Delta turn extremely noisy and lively

The Yellow River carries a large quantity of sand and silt and roars through until it gushes into Bohai Bay, creating the Yellow River Delta Wetland—the youngest soil.

in the migratory season, with red-crowned cranes dancing in shallow waters, whooper swans pluming their feathers elegantly, and all kinds of wild ducks chasing each other freely. Smaller water fowls busily search for food on the beach, while larger ones, such as egrets, cormorants and seagulls, hover over the waves, sometimes in flocks of thousands. Each year, several million migratory birds arrive at the Yellow River Delta for layover on their long, harsh journey, taking a safe, comfortable break.

The muddy beach of the Bohai Bay is the newest land

The boundless reed marshes

just "seized" by the aggressive Yellow River, as just a few months ago this area was still part of the sea. The sea was obviously reluctant to "retreat," as it had left behind many salt water ponds on the beach. The salt water makes it impossible for most plants to grow, and only a few weeds that can resist such salt and alkali have managed to survive.

The real "battlefield" of the land and sea is the Yellow River Wharf. Standing on the pier looking straight ahead, distinguishing between the river water and sea water is very difficult, as both are the same yellow hue. The long pier bridge stretches several hundred meters into the bay, and the surging yellow waves under the bridge that abound with sand and silt faithfully carry out the mission of land reclamation.

Sunrise at the Yellow River Delta

Geological Wonders

The Lunan Stone Forest: Natural Stone Sculptures

Unusual stone peaks, oddly shaped stone columns, and standing stone "shoots" as sharp as knives—all these exist in the Lunan Stone Forest, which has an abundance of intriguing stones and is thus reputed to be a "museum of natural stone sculptures."

A typical example of the karst landform, the Lunan Stone Forest rises straight from the ground to form an amazing spectacle.

Stone columns in the Stone Forest look like bamboo shoots breaking the earth after a spring rain.

The Stone Forest is in Lunan County, some 89 km from Kunming, capital of Yunnan Province. In an area of more than 400 sq. km is a concentration of numerous stone columns, stone "shoots" and stone peaks that look like a forest and thus are named the "Lunan Stone Forest." If the gray limestones in the forest are regarded as "natural sculptures," then Mother Nature is a great sculptor who uses wind, rain, snow and frost as her hammer and chisel. Some stone columns in the Stone Forest are as tall as 30 to 40 meters, rising straight from the ground with dense, delicate lines carved out by water on them. Some stones take the shape of bamboo shoots, with varied heights ranging from 3 or 5 meters to 20 or 30 meters. The stone "shoots" have a thick base but a thin and sharp tip, sometimes as sharp as a saber blade, pointing to the sky. There are also a large array of tall, huge stone peaks in the Stone Forest, which look just like clusters of swords.

The Stone Forest features a typical karst landform in

terms of geological structure. It has taken hundreds of millions of years for this landform to come into being. More than 200 million years ago, the Stone Forest region was a vast sea area, and sediment gradually accumulated on the seabed to form thick limestone layers. Later on, due to the crustaceous movements, the sea floor rose and sank twice and brought the limestone rocks out of the sea about two million years ago. Since then, the originally flat limestone rocks have endured the constant corrosion and erosion by wind and rains, first developing cracks and then breaking into pieces. With water flowing down and penetrating the limestone layers, the stone peaks and columns appeared, and those stones that had undergone more severe weathering turned into stone buds and stone "shoots."

Walking along the narrow paths in the Stone Forest is like wandering around an art museum. Numerous giant rocks stand up from the ground with thousands of

The Ashima Peak

different aspects. People have concocted beautiful legends of the stones in line with their shapes and appearance, the most famous of which is the legend of the Ashima Peak.

On the rim of the Stone Forest, the Ashima Peak resembles a pretty teenaged girl carrying a flower basket on her back, when viewed from a specific angle. The legend says that the stone is the petrified figure of Ashima, a girl of the Sani ethnic group in China. It has almost become a must for visitors to the Stone Forest to have a picture taken with the Ashima Peak in the background, as a precious souvenir.

While the Ashima Peak is undisputedly the jewel of the Lunan Stone Forest, the scenic area also boasts many other "sculptural masterpieces," such as the Camel Peak and Elephant Stone. At Lunan, the great wonders created by nature will always be held in awe.

Wulingyuan: Thousands of Cliffs in Competition With Each Other

More than 3,000 thin and high peaks rise straight from the ground, like gigantic stone columns pointing to the sky. The unique landscape at Wulingyuan is so amazing that the region was put on the UN world natural heritage list in 1992.

Hidden in the deep mountains of northwest Hunan Province, the Wulingyuan scenic area boasts a "jungle" of rocky peaks. Several thousand stone peaks, with varied

The quartz sandstone peaks, erecting straight with sharp edges and corners, form the unique landscape of Wulingyuan.

Due to the humid weather, the peaks at Wulingyuan are often shrouded in white cloud and mist, as if in a traditional Chinese ink painting of landscape.

The Jinbian Stream, one of the most beautiful parts of the Wulingyuan Scenic Area With a total length of 5 to 6 kilometers, the stream winds through mountains and ravines and is famous for its pure, clean water.

heights, ranging from 12 meters to 300 or 400 hundred meters, stand on the ground vertically like clusters of long, slender stone pillars.

The stone peaks at Wulingyuan have cliffs on almost every side, which have some green plants growing in the cracks. The peaks boast various odd shapes; some stand alone like a finger pointed to the sky and others stand shoulder to shoulder as though comparing heights. Some twin peaks have connecting bases but the tops are separated by a narrow gap, as though cleaved with a sharp ax.

Some rocky peaks are so close to each other that only a narrow path that allows one person to pass through exists between them. But other peaks are so far from each other that plenty of ravines, streams, ponds and waterfalls lie between them. The region also has an abundance of precious, ancient trees and restless animals.

Due to the humidity at Wulingyuan, white clouds and mists often plume from the rocky peaks, shrouding them occasionally. From an aerial view, however, many dark-gray stone columns can be seen protruding from the base of the cloud, and look like plants in a forest trying desperately to rise higher as they vie with one another for more sunshine.

The rocks forming the stone peaks at Wulingyuan are quartz sandstones, which are dark and very hard, with sharp edges and corners. The Wulingyuan region is covered with a quartz sandstone layer over 500 meters thick, which is invulnerable to weathering but can develop natural, vertical cracks.

Weather's elements, such as wind, frost, rain and snow, have taken advantage of the natural cracks to grind the hard quartz sandstones, constantly deepening and expanding them until the thick sandstone layer split into numerous stone pillars. However, unlike many other kinds of rocks, the quartz sandstones will never yield to nature's battering and do not lose their sharp features; they either collapse or continue to stand straight. As a result, the unique landscape of "thousands of cliffs in competition with each other" has come into existence at Wulingyuan after a lengthy process of geological evolution.

The Yuanmou Clay Forest: A Golden Palace of Gods

The Clay Forest is a natural wonder that has brought fame to Yuanmou County of Yunnan Province. The region abounds with "clay architecture" in various shapes and forms, with some as large as a castle and some others as small as a tower or a pillar. Yellow is the trademark color of the Clay Forest, but not the only one. Xu Xiake, a famous traveler in China's Ming Dynasty, once said that entering the Clay Forest was an experience of "finding yourself on a golden soil surrounded by colorful clouds."

The "clay" in the Clay Forest is actually rock, a sandstone rock mixed with clay that is yellow, soft and

The natural wonder of clay forest

loose. The rock looks like clay due to serious weathering of its surface. In the sun, the yellow rocks glitter brilliantly as if made of gold. The Clay Forest landscape exists widely in the Yuanmou Basin, with different characteristics for different regions due to the varying levels of corrosion and weathering. The three most famous regions with a typical Clay Forest landscape are Tiger-Leaping Beach, Banguo and Xinhua, each with its own features.

The Clay Forest landscape at Tiger-Leaping Beach is the most magnificent in the Yuanmou area. Observed from afar, the area looks like an abandoned ancient castle, with huge and standing "stone pillars" and stretching "palace walls." The most special feature of the "castle" is that it is capped in clay in a triple color of red, brown and black, resembling the eaves of manmade architecture. The clay

The rock columns in the clay forest have different shapes and colors. What's particularly special is that they often have a "cap" on their top for self-protection.

The clay forest at Banguo glitters in the sunshine.

capping is actually a thick, hard, waterproof layer of iron and calcium, exposed after other parts of the rocks have been corroded by weathering. The capping serves as a "natural shield" for rocks beneath it, playing a key role in preserving the original look of the "castle" at Tiger-Leaping Beach.

With a total area of 14 sq. km, the Clay Forest landscape at Banguo is the largest of its kind in Yuanmou. The Banguo Clay Forest mainly consists of "clay columns" and "clay peaks," which are small in number and sparsely scattered. As the rocks contain light-reflecting minerals, such as agate shreds and sand, the Clay Forest at Banguo shines and glistens under the sun, as though it is decorated with numerous gems.

The Clay Forest at Xinhua has a concentration of tall, huge rocks, and boasts rich colors. Most of the "clay columns" in the region are purple or red on top, gray or white in the middle, and dark or light yellow at the base. The columns present even richer colors when the light changes, like a natural abstract painting. The rich colors of the Clay Forest are related to various minerals in the rocks, which have been exposed after lengthy weathering.

Actually, the Clay Forest landscape has emerged as a result of the long weathering of a large area of rocks, which in the process have gradually lost their soft, loose parts while retaining the hard and solid areas. As the process of weathering and corrosion continues, the Clay Forest of Yuanmou, hailed as a "golden palace of gods," experiences changes every year, a fact that has given the place an everlasting charm.

Zhijin Cave: An Underground Treasure House

In Bijie in west Guizhou Province, Zhijin Cave is a natural cave with gorgeous scenery and a rich variety of sediment.

The size of Zhijin Cave is truly impressive. With a not-so-impressive 15-meter-high, 20-meter-wide entrance halfway up a hill in Zhijin County, Zhijin Cave is extremely spacious inside. The explored section of the cave stretches 12.1 km, consisting of five sub-caves on four tiers and covering a total of 700,000 sq. meters.

Twelve large chambers and 47 small chambers make up this magnificent underground palace; the largest is the "100,000 Mountains Chamber," which covers nearly 70,000 sq. meters, equal to 10 football fields. The chambers also boast an average height of 60 to 100 meters, with the highest measuring 150 meters—equal to a 50-storey building. The landscape in these broad chambers is as

The gorgeous, spacious Zhijin Cave

The Silver Rain Tree

fabulous as that in a miniature world, with some parts as flat as a plain, and others featuring "high peaks," "rivers" and "lakes."

The enormous Zhijin Cave is full of "treasures," and cave explorers describe it as "a treasure house exclusively for God's collections." More than 40 types of sediment found in the world's karst caves exist in Zhijin Cave, in such a variety of forms and shapes as stone "shoots," stone columns, stone pagodas and stone flowers. Among them, two stone "shoots," the Silver Rain Tree and the Helmet of King Warrior, are the crown jewels of the cave, which can hardly be found in any other karst caves in the world.

The Silver Rain Tree is actually a petal-shaped stone "shoot" that keeps growing, with each petal on the 17-meter-high silver "tree" formed by semi-transparent crystals of a milky color. The "tree" grows in a natural "white jade plate" of a two-meter-plus diameter, and looks dazzlingly beautiful and graceful. Geological study shows that this special "tree" has grown 150,000 years to reach its current height, and it is called a "national treasure" of China.

Standing opposite the Silver Rain Tree, the Helmet

The Helmet of King Warrior

of King Warrior is a thick stone "shoot" shaped like an ancient warrior's helmet. On top of a helmet-shaped rock stand two parallel stone pillars, like plumage.

The amazing geological treasures stored in beautiful Zhijin Cave are proof of the lengthy evolution of the earth, which await further exploration and study by the people.

Wu'erhe: Residence of Devils

In an arid and barren desert in the heartland of the Asian continent lies an earthen yellow city, which boasts tall and low "buildings" and flat, twisted roads. There are no residents in the city, but sad and shrill screams can be heard from the city whenever a heavy wind blows across the desert. Some people have thought that this city might be the residence of devils, and named it the "Devil City."

Devil City is located at Wu'erhe Town, which lies in north Xinjiang and on the rim of the Junggar Basin. It is a large area of uneven, crisscrossing earth hills and ridges on the desolate gobi, which looks like an abandoned, ancient city but actually is pure and natural with no artificial traces.

There are also, of course, no devils in the city. In geography, this unique landform is called *yardang*, a Uygur word that means "steep hills." It is a landform caused by wind erosion in an arid, windy environment, and exists in the dry areas of China's Xinjiang and Gansu.

Wu'erhe has a special yardang landform caused by wind erosion. The region is dominated by earth hills in various bizarre shapes.

Wu'erhe looks unique and beautiful in the sunset.

In the Cretaceous Period some 100 million years ago, the Junggar Basin today was an enormous lake, with an abundance of plants on its banks. Unearthed fossils show that many species of dinosaurs, such as the Wu'erhe stegosaurus, plesiosaur and Junggar pterosaur, lived in this region in ancient times. However, after two major crustacean movements, the lake disappeared with its floor lifting to become land.

In the following tens of thousands of years, scorching

suns, strong winds and heavy rains have made this originally flat, solid land full of ditches and gullies, and left the exposed stone layers in various, unusual shapes. As Wu'erhe is a region prone to gales and gusts, the strong winds often carry sand and stones to batter the land, like a sculptor working on marble with hammer and chisel. As a result, all the soft and weak parts of the earth have worn away, with the remaining steep or round earth hills and clusters of earth ridges looking like "earth sculptures" in various bizarre shapes.

In the Devil City, no signs of life can be found, save a few clusters of gray desert plants. Yellow earth hills can be seen in various shapes everywhere, all in dead silence. However, when a wind blows, some weird and even scary whistling sounds will come from nowhere and linger for a long time in the city. The sounds are actually caused by air currents squeezing their way through the coarse rocks in the city, while the standing earth hills and ridges serve as a huge, natural amplifier to make the sounds louder when the wind grows stronger.

When a wind blows, weird and scary whistling sounds will come from nowhere, as if ghosts are screaming. People call this place "the Devil City."

Guilin: A Beautiful Legend of a Thousand Years

The beauty of the landscape at Guilin has long been recognized and eulogized by the Chinese. Those lovely small hills and the river surrounding them have become a beautiful legend passed on from one generation to another over the past 1,000 years.

Located in the north mountainous region of Guangxi Zhuang Autonomous Region, Guilin boasts an unmatched landscape of beautiful peaks. The hills here are neither tall nor large, but they have a special charm with their fantastic shapes and an abundance of unusual stones and enigmatic karst caves. A river as clear and pure as a mirror, the Lijiang River winds through the hills of Guilin. With green mountains, pure rivers, intriguing caves and unusual stones as its most outstanding

The Lijiang River is the soul of the Guilin landscape.

The Elephant Hill represents a typical hill of Guilin.

characteristics, Guilin has enjoyed the reputation as "a place with the world's most beautiful landscape" for thousands of years.

The Lijiang River, which originates in northeast Guilin and flows across Guilin City and the ancient town of Yangshuo, embodies the soul of the Guilin landscape. The 84-km section of the Lijiang River between Guilin and Yangshuo boasts the best scenery and is thus called "a golden waterway."

Like a blue silk ribbon, the Lijiang River flows slowly on the "golden waterway," while hundreds of hills line up on both banks like models in a beauty pageant posing for judges. Elephant Hill represents a typical hill of Guilin. At the convergence of the Lijiang River and Peach Blossoms River (a main tributary of the Lijiang River), the hill received its name for looking like a giant elephant standing still in the water. Local legends say that the elephant, which came to drink from the river, turned itself into a stone hill because it was enchanted with the beautiful landscape.

As a matter of fact, however, all hills at Guilin, including Elephant Hill, are the creation of Mother Nature. The region was a vast sea about three million

In a sunny day, the Lijiang River mirrors each hill on its banks to the point of striking clarity.

years ago, with the seabed covered by a thick layer of limestone. Due to the crustacean movement, the seabed was lifted to become land, and the limestone layer was distorted and broken in the process. Over a lengthy period of geological evolution, various factors, including hot weather and plenty of rainfall, have combined to further transform the rock layer into a complicated karst landform, which features standing peaks on the ground, deep and mysterious caves in the hills, and twisted, crisscrossing hidden rivers underground.

Throughout all seasons and in all weather, the Guilin landscape remains delightful and exhilarating. On clear days, the Lijiang River mirrors each hill on its banks to the point of striking clarity, imparting the sense of sailing on top of the hills while boating on the river. On rainy days, all of the Lijiang River and the neighboring hills are enshrouded in a curtain of rain and light mist, presenting the visitors with a special feeling of "touring a dreamland."

The Yellow Dragon Ravine: A Huge Dragon Hidden in Deep Mountains

In the mountains of the Aba Tibetan Autonomous Prefecture of Sichuan Province lies a "Chinese dragon" developed by natural rocks—with yellow rocks forming its body, water flowing like shining scales, and multi-hued water ponds lying on top of the rocky mountain like eyes. This marvelous area is called the Yellow Dragon Ravine.

The mountain at Yellow Dragon Ravine abounds with yellow rocks, with a 30- to 170-meter-wide rock belt stretching over 3,600 meters from the base to the top, falling over more than 400 meters, like a yellow dragon winding through the valley and climbing the mountain. According to local legend, a flying yellow dragon once landed on the mountain ridge to rest, but became so

There are more than 3,400 colored ponds at the Yellow Dragon Ravine, all with low banks and shallow water.

The travertine beach at the Yellow Dragon Ravine stretches for about 1,300 meters, the longest and largest of its kind ever found in the world.

intoxicated by the beautiful scenery that it decided to stay forever to guard this region.

Actually, the special yellow rocks at Yellow Dragon Ravine are called travertine, which is a rare geological phenomenon created by the coalescence of limestone and water. Limestone abounds in the Yellow Dragon Ravine region, while snow water from the surrounding high mountains and other surface water seep through the limestone layers, resulting in calcium carbonate. The groundwater rich in calcium carbonate then flows into the streams through estuaries or cracks in the rocks. Due to the rapid drop of water temperature and pressure, the calcium carbonate separates from the water in the form of white crystals—the travertine, that, after mixing with impure substances such as soil, results in a dark or light yellow.

Travertine can be found everywhere at the Yellow Dragon Ravine; there are travertine ponds, travertine

A close-up of the Yellow Dragon Ravine colored ponds

streams, travertine caves and travertine springs. Even tree branches and leaves that have fallen into the streams are covered by a hard shell of travertine, lying in the water like sculptures.

The most beautiful part of the Yellow Dragon Ravine is Five-Color Ponds, which lies at the highest point of the whole travertine area and is dubbed "eyes of the yellow dragon." The largest of its kind in the whole scenic area, Five-Color Ponds comprise several hundred large and small travertine ponds of various colors. Water flows over the low banks of these ponds, which look like beautiful jade plates in colors of red, purple, blue and green in the sunshine.

The Yellow Dragon Ravine boasts the world's largest travertine waterfall, travertine streams and highland travertine ponds. As sedimentation of calcium is a very slow process, geologists believe that it has taken more than 30,000 years for the Yellow Dragon Ravine to become what it looks like today.

Yeliu: A Sculpture Park on the Coast

Sea waves also act a sculptor when they arrive at Yeliu.

A narrow, long cape on northern Taiwan island, Yeliu has a wonderful "sculpture park," with a host of stone sculptures in various shapes and designs scattered on the coast.

The Yeliu cape, or a narrow strip of rocks intruding into the sea, has a length of more than 1,600 meters. Due to sea wave erosion and weathering, a rich landform of marine abrasion has formed at Yeliu. The formation of the unusual natural sculptures at Yeliu can be traced back more than 20 million years, when the Taiwan island known today was still submerged in the sea. The sand washed out from today's Chinese mainland gathered here and gradually formed a sandstone layer. The orogenesis, or the process of mountain formation some 6 million years ago, lifted the sea floor and the Taiwan island emerged. Sea water then continuously eroded the sandstone layer, leading to

A Beauty's Head (Queen's Head) "sculpture" on the coast of Yeliu, a result of continuous erosion by sea waves.

The special sea erosion landform at Yeliu

what people see at Yeliu today.

People have named the rocks on the Yeliu coast according to their shapes, such as the mushroom rocks, ginger rocks and beancurd rocks. The mushroom rocks are the most special among all rocks at Yeliu. With a height of one to four meters, these stones resemble mushrooms, with a thin base and a thick head, looking like a big, heavy "stone head" supported by a short, thin "stone neck." The most famous mushroom rock is called the "Queen's Head," which is composed of a very slender stone neck and a top with a close resemblance of the head of a western noblewoman in a fashionable hairstyle.

The head of a mushroom rock is actually formed by the remains of ancient marine life such as seashells. The

calcium in their shells accumulated in the rocks and formed a hard core. In the process of weathering, the comparatively soft sandstone was eroded and the calcium hard core once wrapped in the sandstone gradually became exposed, eventually becoming unique "stone sculptures." With continuing erosion by sea waves and the rising earth crust, the "stone neck" of the mushroom rock will continue to weather and become thinner and thinner, until it can no longer hold the weight of the "stone head" and finally collapses.

The different shapes of the original calcium hard cores have led to the different "designs" and appearances of the stone sculptures. The candlestick rocks are another kind of famous stone on the Yeliu coast. They look like candle holders, with a round and protruding base, a comparatively thin middle section, and a slightly sunken top. Some of the rocks even have a twist at the top that looks like a candle flame. There are also rocks at Yeliu that have distorted under geological pressure and developed many cracks due to the continuous washing of sea waves. These rocks are called the "ginger rocks" as the two look very much alike.

There are also many other strange rocks on the Yeliu coast. On the flat surface of some rocks exists a deep, round hole, with a small mouth but spacious interior. The hole has a round stone inside and is filled with sea water. Such well-like holes came into existence by accident: the sea water accidentally pushed a stone into a sunken part of the rock, and the stone, carried by the sea water, ground the rock every day until a hole was created and continuously enlarged.

At Yeliu many relics of life forms can also be seen, as well as beautiful fossils of sea hedgehogs and starfishes and fossils that have recorded traces of ancient reptiles. These relics and fossils are not only precious materials for scientific research, but charming, lovely decorations of the Yeliu coast.

Colorful Eco-Systems

The Tropical Rain Forest in Xishuangbanna: A Wild Jungle

Monkeys jump on treetops, wild elephants roam on jungle paths, tigers hide in bushes waiting for prey, and pythons slither through the forest... This is a jungle world full of wilderness—the tropical rain forest in Xishuangbanna.

The buttress root

Located on the south borders of China and in the mountainous region of south Yunnan Province, Xishuangbanna boasts the largest, best-preserved rain forest in the country. The weather here is warm and humid year long, and the place has plenty of sunshine, pure, winding rivers and dense, mysterious jungles.

The tall trees in the jungle block the sunlight, and all trees strive to grow higher, vying with each other for more sunshine. In order to better support themselves and absorb

The killer of a gigantic tree. It is quite common in a rain forest that the strangler plants, with a net of numerous aerial roots, smother a gigantic tree which used to support their growth.

more nutrients, the gigantic arbor trees have developed a special buttress root, or several pieces of triangular extensions from the bottom of the trunk. The buttress root is a dozen to scores of centimeters thick, and sometimes as tall as four to five meters, thus looking spectacular. Several pieces of buttress root form a stable base for a huge tree, which is so thick that even a dozen people joining their arms cannot embrace it. From a vantage point at the base of the tree, only the crown of the tree can be seen stretching far into the sky.

Not all the plants in the jungle can grow tall and

The wild elephants in the jungle of Xishuangbanna

huge, so some have adopted a cruel means of survival —strangling. Such plants, for example, the banyan trees, first have their seeds swallowed by birds and beasts and then wait for the seeds to be discharged onto the branches of other trees along with the animals' excrement. Supported by nutrients in the excrement and branch scraps, the seeds can sprout and grow. The banyan tree can develop multiple tube-shaped aerial roots, which hang in the air to absorb water and continue growing downward. Such aerial roots have become a common sight in the jungle, which hang from the high, enormous tree crowns and sway in the air. Upon touching the ground, the aerial roots will immediately take root and grow increasingly thicker and stronger. When a banyan tree becomes fully grown, the original tree that supported its growth is tightly entangled with its aerial roots, which can easily smother the original tree.

There are also some plants that have no great ambition and are content with "standing on the shoulders of the giants" to share sunshine and rain. Almost every tall tree in the rain forest has various parasitic plants growing on it. Seen from the base of the trees, the tree trunks appear to be "decorated" either with a huge "flower ball" or a delicate "bird's nest." These are actually ferns leading a parasitic life, which have built splendid "gardens in the air," one after another.

Compared with the plants, animals in the jungle tend to lead low-key lives and hide themselves carefully. Therefore, more patience is required to see them. Currently more than 500 kinds of land-based vertebrate animals, or nearly one-fourth of the total species found in China, have been found in the Xishuangbanna rain forest. The Indian elephant, Indochinese tiger, white-cheeked gibbon, green peacock, lesser panda, slow laris, and many other unknown species of animals lead happy lives in the rain forest, in accord with long-respected jungle rules.

The Bamboo Sea in Southern Sichuan: A Tranquil World of Bamboo

The bamboo sea is a world of bamboo. When a breeze blows, tens of thousands of bamboo dance like surging waves of the sea.

The bamboo sea is located in the extension of the Liantian Mountain in south Sichuan Province, with a total area of 120 sq. km. More than 20 mountain ridges and over 500 peaks and hills in the region are all covered with bamboo. The boundless bamboo sea is so intoxicating that Huang Tingjian, a famous poet of the Song Dynasty, was deeply touched and left the inscription "Wan Ling Qing," which means "large groves of bamboo on 10,000 mountains."

The majority of bamboo in the Southern Sichuan Bamboo Sea is the Nanzhu bamboo, a common species of bamboo that can be found in many parts of China. Nanzhu bamboo is tall and upright, and often gather

A sea of bamboo

densely together in a grove. Wandering in a Nanzhu grove, the sight of smooth bamboo stems reflecting sunshine can be enjoyed, along with the unique fragrance of bamboo leaves and the sound of the "whispers" of bamboo leaves shivering in the breeze.

Besides the Nanzhu bamboo, which can be seen everywhere, the bamboo sea also accommodates more than 50 other kinds of bamboo, which all have their own characteristics. The black bamboo is an "alien" of the bamboo family; light green with dense, tiny hairs on its stem when it is young, and gradually turning dark purple and even ink black when it is fully grown. The black bamboo is not tall and looks delicate in the green sea of bamboo. The fishpole bamboo has small but dense leaves, and the greatest characteristic of this bamboo lies in its joints—the joints of the upper half are straight and regularly shaped, but the joints close to the ground are

A breeze will stir up "green waves" in the bamboo sea.

unique and delightful in all different, irregular shapes. Also growing in the bamboo sea are peaceful fishscale bamboo, pretty Chinese goddess bamboo, and Chinese affinity bamboo, which feature the co-existence of adult and baby bamboo. Many bamboo in the bamboo sea belong to rare and precious species.

The bamboo is a favorite plant in traditional Chinese culture. With such features as being hollow and upright and remaining green in all seasons, the bamboo are often personalized and taken as a symbol of personal integrity and righteousness by Chinese artists and gentlemen in ancient times. Many people believe that a tour in the bamboo sea can help them better understand the essence of life, and that they have much to learn from the bamboo, say, the unyielding spirit of the old bamboo and the pioneering spirit of bamboo sprout, the lofty pursuit of the tall bamboo and the humility and confidence of short bamboo.

No matter how seasons change and how people view it, the Southern Sichuan Bamboo Sea is always green and tranquil, lying still in deep mountains.

The Diverse-Leaf Poplar Forest in Luntai: Heroic Trees in the Desert

The diverse-leaf poplar forest lies beside the desert, with endless dunes and extreme aridity being its sole company. In this harsh environment, the diverse-leaf poplar trees have managed to survive and prosper, making everyone marvel at their strong life force and thus earning the fame as "heroic trees in the desert."

The Luntai region of China's Xinjiang Uygur Autonomous Region boasts the world's largest and densest diverse-leaf poplar forest. The natural forest covers more than 400,000 mu (26,666 hectares), stretching along Tarim River, which flows across Taklimakan Desert.

The diverse-leaf poplar forest in Luntai—a symbol of life and endurance

The diverse-leaf poplar is called "Tok-rak" in Uygur, which literally means "the most beautiful tree." It is really an extraordinary tree, as an old saying goes: "The diverse-leaf poplar could live for 1,000 years, stand for another 1,000 years after its death, and remain unrotten for yet another 1,000 years after its fall." To withstand freezing cold, extreme heat and strong winds in the desert, the diverse-leaf poplar trees are mostly thick and sturdy, with a five- to six-meter-high tree having a trunk of a one-meter diameter. As straight trunks are vulnerable to wind erosion, most diverse-leaf poplar trees have twisted trunks that grow all kinds of strange shapes. The crown of the tree is as dense as a lid, while the leaves are small and delicate—typical features of desert trees in response to the arid climate. Even mid-summer, the

The diverse-leaf poplar forest is full of vitality thanks to the irrigation of the Tarim River.

leaves of the diverse-leaf poplar won't yield any green, which protects them from the sizzling sun. In autumn, however, the leaves will suddenly turn golden as if they want to display the glory of life with such a splendid color.

The diverse-leaf poplar forest is located in the heartland of the Taklimakan Desert, stretching along the Tarim River.

Seen from a high perspective, the Tarim River winds through the desert with numerous tributaries. The diverse-leaf poplar trees grow between the courses of the river and tributaries, and stretch far into the desert. Due to the severe lack of water in the desert, the poplar trees are largely scattered, either standing alone or existing in small groups of two or three. The blue river reflects the sky, and the golden poplar grows by the sand dune, the picturesque scene not only feasting the eyes, but conveying the profound meaning of life.

The diverse-leaf poplar forest of Luntai nurtures the heroic trees in the desert, and demonstrates the beauty of life and persistence.

The Changbai Mountain Forest: Virgin Forest in North China

The Changbai Mountain is in northeast China, and its west slope has a precious reserve of a mixed virgin forest, which mainly consists of coniferous trees such as Korean pines, as well as broad-leaf trees. All the trees co-exist peacefully and grow lushly in the mountain, fully displaying the beauty of north China forests.

The Korean pine grows not only on the slopes but in the valleys and ravines. The forest is permeated with the special fragrance of pine trees. Sunshine pierces through the treetop to reach the bottom of the forest and nurture the vegetation there. The ground is covered by a thick layer of lichen, which adds a green coat to both the rocks

The Korean Pine Mixed Virgin Forest adds enormous charm to the Changbai Mountain.

and exposed tree roots. The forest boasts a special black soil that can only be found in northeast China. The black soil is rich in compost and extremely fertile, providing sufficient nutrients for all plants growing in the forest.

Among tens of thousands of Korean pines in the forest is a famous "Pine King," which is more than 480 years old and over 35 meters high. It takes three adults joining their arms to fully embrace the tree. Even more amazing is the fact that the "Pine King" has survived three volcanic eruption of the Changbai Mountain over the past 300 years, though it is not too far from the crater; many believe this is simply a miracle.

The Korean pine has a highly developed root system that can store a large quantity of water. The prosperity of the Changbai Mountain Forest can be partly attributed to the Korean pine's role in water conservation. The Korean pine also has a special feature—shade-loving when it is young and sun-loving when it is fully grown. Therefore, the saplings of the Korean pine always live at the bottom of the forest in darkness and shade, while the fully grown pine trees are very tall and always dominate the top of the forest.

Apart from the Korean pine, the forest is also home to many other trees such as spruces, birches and Chinese lindens. Rich plant species have enabled the forest to remain colorful and hardy year long. Though spring falls

The Changbai Mountain Forest in autumn

In winter, the whole forest is turned into a white kingdom by heavy snow.

late in northeast China, the dark-green Korean pines will have already developed new leaves, with new buds already on the bare branches of the broad-leaf trees. In summer, all plants flourish and the forest is shrouded in a light-yellow smog. The yellow smog is actually the pollen released by tens of thousands of Korean pines, as the tree's blossoming season falls at the end of June. The forest looks most beautiful in autumn, with various trees displaying a variety of colors, ranging from emerald and dark green to golden, crimson and silver. In winter, the whole forest is turned into a white kingdom by heavy snow.

The Giant Panda Habitat in Sichuan: Homeland of the Giant Pandas

The giant panda is a wild animal found only in China, mainly in the mountainous regions of Shaanxi, Gansu and Sichuan Provinces. The mountainous region in west Sichuan has been listed by

A giant panda living in the dense forest

The Siguniang Mountain is a sacred mountain to the local Tibetans. According to the local legends, there were four beautiful and kind-hearted girls in the ancient times who fought ferocious leopards to protect the lovely giant pandas and later turned into four erecting peaks—the Siguniang Mountain today.

UNESCO as a site of world natural heritage, as it is home to a large number of giant pandas living in the wild and serves as a main habitat for this endangered species.

The giant panda resembles a bear, with its body and tail being white but limbs, ears and eye lined in black. It has a big, round head and fat body, as well as a very short tail, which makes it appear unusual and cute. Though it looks clumsy and slow, the giant panda is agile and quick, especially at climbing trees.

An ancient animal that has survived the vicissitudes of time and space, the giant panda witnessed the peak period of species prosperity more than one million years ago. At that time, they were widely scattered in today's southeast China, ranking among the main animal species on earth along with stegodons, an extinct elephant-like mammal, and smilodons, or saber-toothed tigers. However, with the arrival of the Quaternary Ice Age, the climatic conditions on earth changed drastically and led to the successive extinction of other animals of the same period. The areas where the giant pandas lived also kept dwindling, and finally the animal's activities were confined to the small, narrow regions of the Hengduan

The Wolong region—homeland of the giant pandas

Mountains and Qinling Mountains in west China. At present, the population of the giant panda is so small—less than 2,000 both in the wild and in captivity—that the animal has become one of the most endangered species in the world.

The giant panda is a predator, according to zoological classification. However, in order to adapt themselves to the environment over their long history, they have changed their diet from meat to bamboo, becoming "vegetarian bears" that only catch and eat small animals like bamboo rats occasionally. As the giant panda has maintained the basic characteristics of a predator, such as highly developed canine teeth and short intestines, it is reputed as a "living fossil" in animals.

Sichuan is the most important habitat for wild giant pandas, with 9,510 sq. km of mountainous regions, including the narrow mountain belt between the Dadu River and Minjiang River, the Wolong region, the

Siguniang Mountain and the Jiajin Mountain range, highlighted on the "world natural heritage" list. More than 30 percent of the wild giant pandas in the world live in this region, making it the world's largest and most integrated giant panda habitat.

The heartland of the Sichuan giant panda habitat is the region of Wolong and Siguniang Mountain, which is home to approximately 300-plus giant pandas. The region belongs to the Hengduan mountain system, which boasts snow-capped high peaks, lush vegetation at the base of the mountains, and large areas of natural forest. Therefore, the region has preserved multiple eco-systems with typical characteristics of the subtropical, temperate and frigid zones, has nurtured the second richest plant species only after the rain forest, and has provided an ideal home for wild animals. Apart from the giant panda, the region also houses such rare and endangered animals as golden hair monkey, snow leopard and white-lipped deer. No wonder the region has been listed as one of the 25 ecological-hotspot regions in the world by international wildlife protection organizations.

Hoh Xil Highland Wildlife Habitat: A Paradise in No Man's Land

Hoh Xil, which has a climate too harsh for mankind to endure for long, is a paradise for wildlife. It is one of the most important habitats for highland wild animals in the world, for it has a well-preserved, unique plateau eco-system.

Located in the plateau area between the Kunlun Mountains and the Ulan Ul Mountain, Hoh Xil has an average elevation of 4,500 to 5,000 meters. There are two mountains in Hoh Xil, namely the Hoh Xil Mountain and the Dongbolei Mountain, with a flat and vast lake basin lying between them. Due to the harsh natural conditions, such as high-altitude cold and lack of oxygen, Hoh Xil has witnessed scarce human activities since ancient times.

Hoh Xil, the largest no man's land in China rarely affected by human activities, has largely maintained its primitive appearance. This photo shows the Tuotuo River that flows across Hoh Xil.

It is the largest no man's land in China, as well as one of the best-preserved virgin ecological environments in the country.

The high elevation of Hoh Xil has led to thin air and frigid weather, with the annual average temperature below minus 4 degrees Celsius. Heavy snowfall is possible any time, even mid-summer, while the temperature can drop to minus 40-plus degrees Celsius in winter. Such a harsh environment has posed a severe challenge to the survival of any life form. On the open, vast wasteland no tall vegetation grows, with all kinds of grass scattered sparsely and growing as close to the ground as possible. The grass turns hardy and blossoms beautifully only once every year, in the warmest month, and then resume its yellow-gray again to melt into the general hue of the land.

With a large area covered by glaciers, Hoh Xil boasts all kinds of lakes and seasonal rivers, which form the prettiest scenery here. Plants flourish by the lakes to support the lives of Tibetan antelopes, wild yaks and Tibetan wild donkeys, which, along with predators like wolves, brown bears and vultures, form a complete highland eco-system.

An adult Tibetan antelope has a dark face, with black marks on its legs and harp-shaped horns on its head for self-defense. The Tibetan antelope is called "the pride of Hoh Xil" and has been put under first-class state protection in China.

Tibetan antelope is the most important wild animal under state protection now living in Hoh Xil. This animal has beautiful form and moves swiftly, while the males look even more striking with a pair of dark, shining long horns. The hair of the Tibetan antelope can be made into a famous, precious shawl named Shahtoosh. It is said that the Shahtoosh shawl is so thin and soft that it can easily be pulled through a small ring, thus gaining the nickname of "ring shawls." Seeking high profits, poachers used to slaughter Tibetan antelopes in mass quantities, and the population dropped sharply to the verge

The baby Tibetan antelopes

of extinction. This prompted the local government to severely crack down on poaching activities, while non-governmental organizations also actively protected the endangered species. Now, the number of Tibetan antelopes living in Hoh Xil has begun to rise steadily, and, each summer, large herds of the Tibetan antelopes can be seen on their way to a long-distance migration to find safe, secluded places to breed.

The wild animals are the true masters of Hoh Xil, and they often view humans who enter their region as "intruders." Many people who once drove to Hoh Xil shared this experience: the wild donkeys raced against the car and would not stop until they won, as though they wanted the "intruders" to know who the true "speed champions" were. The wild yaks sometimes were provoked by the car and would try to ram it in a wild rage. Under such circumstances, the only option for the driver was to drive away as quickly as possible, for the car would not be able to withstand the force of a giant animal weighing one ton.

Despite the harsh natural conditions in Hoh Xil, this region is a paradise for wild animals, which are always roaming on the wild highland with a free spirit.

Shennongjia: A Mystic Haven for Wildlife

Shennongjia boasts one of the best-preserved virgin forests in China. It enjoys the fame of "haven for wildlife," as it is home to a large quantity of wildlife, including many ancient species that have survived catastrophic climatic changes on earth.

Shennongjia is in the mountainous area in west-central China's Hubei Province. Covering more than 3,000 sq. km, Shennongjia has high mountains and

Shennongjia has high mountains and deep valleys with lush vegetation, and ranks among the world's best-preserved subtropical forest eco-systems at the same latitude.

deep valleys with lush vegetation, and ranks among the world's best-preserved subtropical forest eco-systems at the same latitude. The unique natural conditions have helped Shennongjia to become a "paradise of species multiplication."

Located in central China, Shennongjia is a zone of transition for plant species in north and south China, and therefore houses a large variety of biological species from different regions and eco-systems. The climatic conditions

The golden hair monkey has a long tail, almost of the same length as its body. The animal boasts golden-color soft, long hairs, the longest of which can exceed 30 centimeters, as if it wears a golden "cloak."

of Shennongjia have undergone little change since the Jurassic Period of Mesozoic, only suffering minor damage during the Ice Age. As a result, many ancient and special plant species have managed to survive. Several thousands of different plants grow in Shennongjia, many of which are extremely rare and precious species now under State protection. They include spinulose tree ferns, which used to be the food of dinosaurs, davidia involucrate, which has beautiful flowers resembling white pigeons, and Chinese Paris rhizome, a medicinal herb with the effect of killing inflammation.

The flourishing plants have provided sufficient food for a rich variety of animal species, helping Shennongjia to boast one of the world's richest subtropical species reserves. The known animal species in Shennongjia include 285 kinds of birds, 77 kinds of beasts, 60 kinds of amphibians and reptiles, and several thousand kinds of insects, while many more unknown species are waiting to be discovered. Shennongjia is home to extremely rare and precious animal species such as the golden hair monkey with bright fur of golden-yellow, and the Chinese Luehdorfia butterfly with flowery wings of dark and yellow.

Shennongjia also ranks among the most mysterious places in China, as the frequent sightings of white animals and the legends of "Big Foot" have put a veil of enigma on this land densely covered by a virgin forest.

With a beautiful landscape and agreeable climate, Shennongjia is a zone of transition for plant species in north and south China, and therefore houses a large variety of biological species from different regions and eco-systems.

People have found many kinds of white animals, ranging from bears, snakes, monkeys and roe deer to muntjacs, magpies, crows and weasels. As it is quite unusual for some animals in nature to turn white due to genetic mutation, the fact that so many white animals exist in Shennongjia has greatly puzzled zoologists.

The legend of "Big Foot," which traces back to long ago in the Shennongjia region, is also one of the best-known natural mysteries in China. To verify the claims by several hundred local villagers that they had seen mysterious human-like animals in the forests, scientists successively launched four field studies in Shennongjia. Though failing to find any "Big Foot" in the dense forests, they discovered traces such as the hair and footprints of unknown animals, causing greater public concern and speculation.

The beautiful, mysterious Shennongjia awaits further exploration. While nurturing numerous known and unknown plants and animals, it also fosters people's curiosity and imagination.

Chengshantou: A Battlefield of Land and Sea

Chengshantou lies at the easternmost point of China's coastline. It was once regarded as the residence of the sun god and therefore frequently visited by ancient emperors who wanted to pay homage to the Sun God.

The Jiaodong Peninsula of China looks like a dagger piercing into the sea, and Chengshantou is located at the tip of the "dagger." It is just like a battlefield of land and sea: the land intrudes into the sea with sword-like giant rocks, while the

Chengshantou is encircled by the sea from three sides. The coastal area features steep crags, ferocious sea waves and swift currents.

sea retaliates with its billowing waves, beating the rocks mercilessly day and night.

Chengshantou, which is now under the jurisdiction of Rongcheng City, Shandong Province, was called "the end of the sky" in ancient times. It is at the easternmost point of China's coastline, marking the eastern end of the Chinese land mass and facing the boundless sea. In the late 3rd century BC, Emperor Qinshihuang, the first feudal emperor in Chinese history who realized the country's complete unification, arrived at Chengshantou to worship the gods of mountains and sea and to look for the legendary "medicine against death." Li Si, a minister serving in Emperor Qinshihuang's court, left an inscription that read "the end of the sky and the eastern gate of the Qin empire." As Chengshantou is the first place on the Chinese mainland to greet sunrises on the sea, historical records show that the ancient Chinese believed it was the residence of the Sun God. In 94 BC, Liu Che, an emperor of the Han Dynasty which replaced the Qin regime, went to Chengshantou to enjoy the sight of sunrise at sea and worship the Sun God, and ordered the construction of a temple dedicated to the Sun God there.

Chengshantou is encircled by the sea from three sides, with a huge, long and narrow yellow rock stretching far into the sea. The rock, standing more than 100 meters above the sea, looks like a giant boat ready to set sail. Sitting on top of the huge rock gives a view of several cone-shaped stone isles emerging from the sea. The color and orientation of the stone isles reveals that they are actually connected with the huge rock. They are like the vanguard of an "invasion force" trying to conquer the sea.

The counterattack of the sea is fierce and persistent, as huge waves keep on beating the rock with a deafening clash. The waves break after hitting the hard rock and turn into white foam drifting below. Strong winds blow across the top of the huge rock year long, creating a whistling as though the wind is also cheering on the battle. Braving the strong winds, salanganes hover in the air and often present a "stunt show," either charging towards the surface of the sea along a vertical route or circling around time and again tirelessly.

At the bottom of the huge rock stands a sign post warning visitors against approaching the sea, though the sea is still several meters away. Actually, the sea waves at Chengshantou are really unpredictable and treacherous.

Most of the time they are only one or two meters high and do not reach the rock, but every several minutes a four or five-meter-high huge wave will come and rage through the beach, taking away everything in a radius of several meters upon its retreat.

Despite the fierce encounter of land and sea at Chengshantou, the sea area far from the place looks tranquil, while the mountains and rivers far behind Chengshantou also remain silent. Through the gaps of clouds the sun casts tens of thousands of golden rays onto the sea's surface, and the mountains also look splendid with colorful trees and flowers. Behind this picture of peace and harmony, both the land and sea are quietly accumulating their forces and preparing for a fresh clash at Chengshantou.

The pure, blue sea water reflects sunlight at Xisha.

The South China Sea Islands: China's Pearl Necklace

South of the vast landmass of China lies a pure blue territory, the South China Sea. Scattered in this immense sea area are numerous coral islands, shoals and hidden reefs, which all form a beautiful pearl necklace along the east coast of the Pacific Ocean.

Geographically speaking, the South China Sea, or literally the "South Sea," refers to the vast sea area south of the Chinese mainland, particularly to the south of the Hainan Island, which stretches all the way to the vicinity of the equator. China has a long history of exploring and

The red-footed booby

developing the South China Sea Islands, as the South China Sea had served as the starting point of China's "maritime silk road" for silk exports to the West since the Han Dynasty dating back more than 2,000 years. In the Ming Dynasty, the famous Chinese seafarer Zheng He and his fleet sailed across the South China Sea to visit many countries in Southeast Asia and Africa. The South China Sea has always served as a major transport, trade and military passage for China.

In the tropical zone, the South China Sea boasts pure blue water with excellent transparency. Swarms of fish swim in the water while flocks of sea birds hover in the sky. According to their geographical locations, the South China Sea Islands are divided into the Dongsha, Xisha,

Sand beach of Xisha

Zhongsha and Nansha Island Groups. The Zengmu Reef marks the southernmost end of the Chinese territory, which is already several thousand km from the coastline of the mainland and not far from Malaysia.

The Dongsha Island Group is the closest island group to the Chinese mainland on the South China Sea, and the second largest island on the South China Sea, the Dongsha Island, belongs here. The island boasts plenty of coconut trees and shining beaches of tiny white sands. On the east and northwest sides of the island lie a Dongsha reef, a Beiwei shoal and a Nanwei shoal, all of which are submerged by the sea but cluster around the Dongsha Island like moons around a planet.

The Xisha Island Group, consisting of a chain of islands, shoals and hidden reefs, is believed to be the most beautiful in all South China Sea Islands. The Yongxing Island of the Xisha Island Group is the largest island on the South China Sea. With an area of 2.8 sq. km, the island is heart-shaped and is thus called "the heart of China." To the east of the Yongxing Island lies a smaller, milky color island, the Dongdao Island, which is 1.6 sq. km. The beaches on the Dongdao Island are piled with the sand of sea shells and corals, and therefore are extremely beautiful. There are a lot of plants and sea birds on the island, with a particularly large population of the red-footed booby. The red-footed boobies, which are very cute with white feathers and crimson feet, are called the "navigation birds" by the local fishermen for their superb instinct of finding land. For this reason, they have become a symbol of the Xisha Island Group.

The Zhongsha Island Group is in the center of the South China Sea Islands. Except for the Huangyan Island, the island group mainly comprises coral shoals and reefs largely submerged by the sea. With clean, pure water and a moderate water temperature of 25 to 28 degrees Celsius, the Zhongsha Island Group provides a perfect environment for the breeding and growth of all kinds of sea lives.

The Nansha Island Group boasts the largest area and the largest number of islands and reefs among the four South China Sea island groups. More than 200 islands, reefs and shoals are scattered in a vast 820,000 sq. km, with the area of the largest island not exceeding a half sq. km. Close to the equator, the island group boasts a typical tropical landscape, and the coral underwater are in all different colors and shapes. Though the Nansha Island Group lies far from the Chinese mainland, it assumes great significance as the "South National Gate" of China.

Appendix: China's General Natural Conditions

China is located in southeast Eurasia and on the west bank of the Pacific. It is the world's third largest country with a land territory of around 9.6 million sq. km. The overwhelming majority of the Chinese territory is situated in the mid-latitude zone. From south to north, the Chinese territory stretches for about 5,500 km from around latitude 4° N to latitude 53° 31' N. From west to east, it extends for some 5,200 km from longitude 73°40'E to longitude 135° 05' E.

With complex and varied climatic conditions, China has both tropical regions that are hot year long, and alpine regions or cold regions that are always covered with snow. Nevertheless, the majority of the Chinese territory lies in the subtropical, warm-temperate and temperate zones, which are well-suited for human habitation with a mild climate and distinct seasons. Lying between the world's largest continent and largest ocean, China has a monsoon climate. Influenced by the alternation of summer and winter monsoons each year, the summer temperatures in China are comparatively higher than those in other regions of the world at the same latitude, while the winter temperatures are comparatively lower. Generally, the country is hot and rainy in summer, and cold and dry in winter.

It is common to divide China's land territory into north and south, or east and west. In terms of climatic changes, the temperature keeps dropping from south to north, and the temperature differences are most remarkable in winter, when the south is still a green world but the north has turned into a snow land. From east to west, the climate turns from humid to dry as the sea grows increasingly distant. The double impact on the climate by latitude and longitude differences has made China's climatic conditions extremely complicated and unpredictable, with great climatic differences between different regions of the country in the same period of time.

China also has a varied topography as it is home to both the world's highest peak 8,844.43 meters above sea level and low lands more than 150 meters below sea level. Lying between the two extremes of altitude are lofty plateaus, extended mountains, heaving hills, mountain-surrounded basins, vast deserts, large plains, and numerous lakes—all displaying the country's rich and colorful land.

A typical feature of China's topography is "highlands in the west and plains in the east." The country's land territory can be divided into three tiers. The Qinghai-Tibet Plateau in China's west forms the highest tier. The Qinghai-Tibet Plateau has an average elevation of 4,500 meters, thus reputed to be "the roof of the world," and its total area accounts for one-fourth of China's land territory. Majestic mountain ranges stand on the plateau, with the world's highest mountain, the Himalayas, on the plateau's south fringe. The snow-capped mountains have nurtured numerous glaciers around them, making China one of the world's leading countries in glacier reserves. These glaciers are the origin of many important rivers that provide a large quantity of fresh water for the country every year.

The vast area north and east of the Qinghai-Tibet Plateau that drops to an elevation of 1,000 to 2,000 meters forms the second tier, a land interspersed with extensive basins and highlands. Here are the rugged Yunnan-Guizhou Plateau, ravine-rich Loess Plateau and rolling Inner Mongolia Plateau, as well as the picturesque Sichuan Basin, mineral-rich Qaidam Basin, and untamed Tarim Basin and Junggar Basin. Multiple land forms include snowy mountains, forests, grasslands and deserts, which co-exist on the second tier.

The third tier consists of plains in northeast and south China and the country's coastal regions, with an average elevation below 1,000 meters. There are fertile plains and rolling small hills in this area, while the northeast China Plain, north China Plain and Yangtze Plain boast the country's most fertile land and best natural conditions, thus having a dense population, developed economy and numerous historical sites.

China also has 3 million sq. km of sea territory to the east and south of its vast land territory. China's sea territory stretches along the east coast of the Pacific and arcs across temperate, subtropical and tropical seas from north to south. China's continental coastline has a total length of more than 18,000 km, and there are about 6,500 large and small islands, which are scattered along the coastline like pearls.

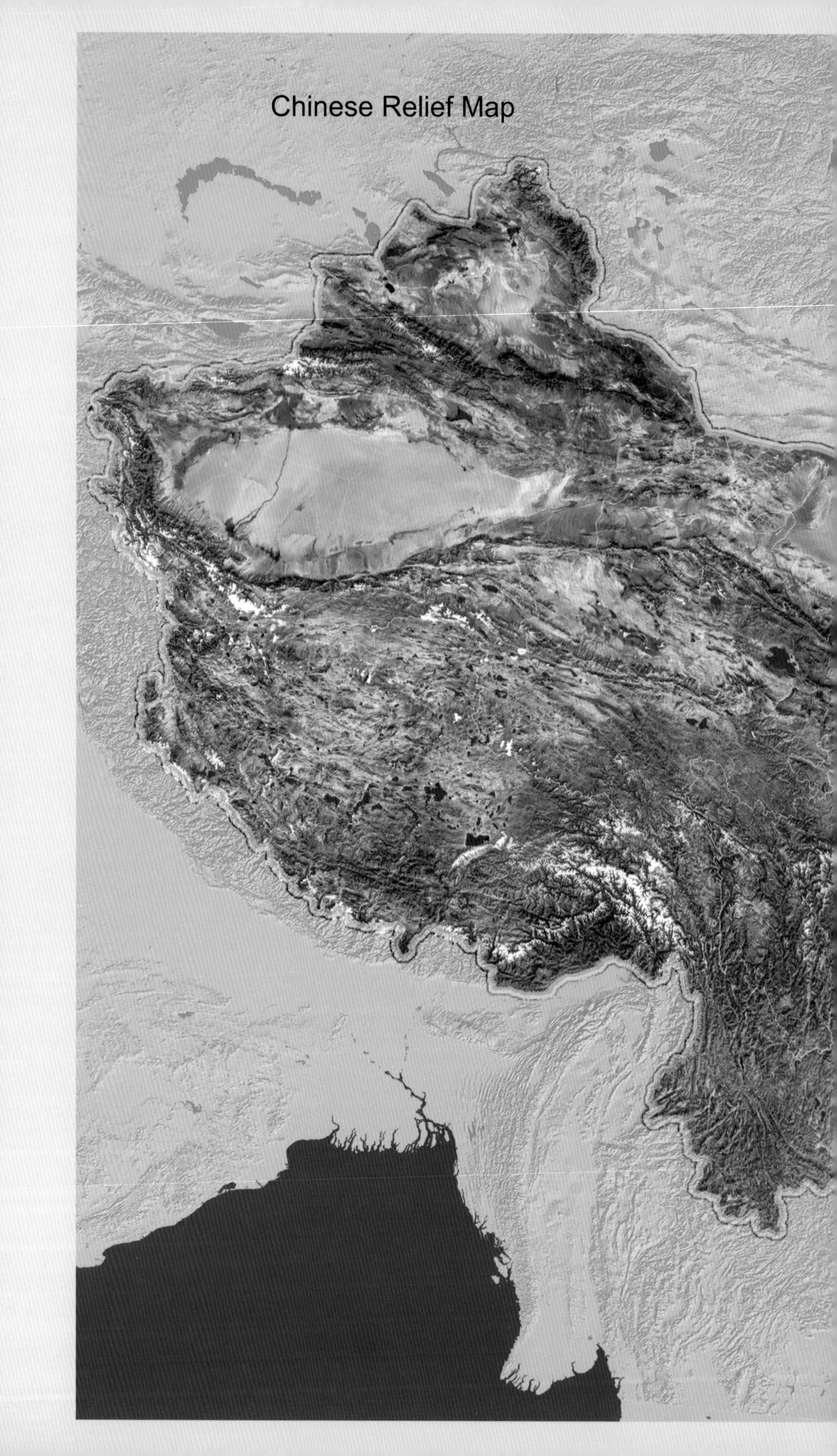
Chinese Relief Map

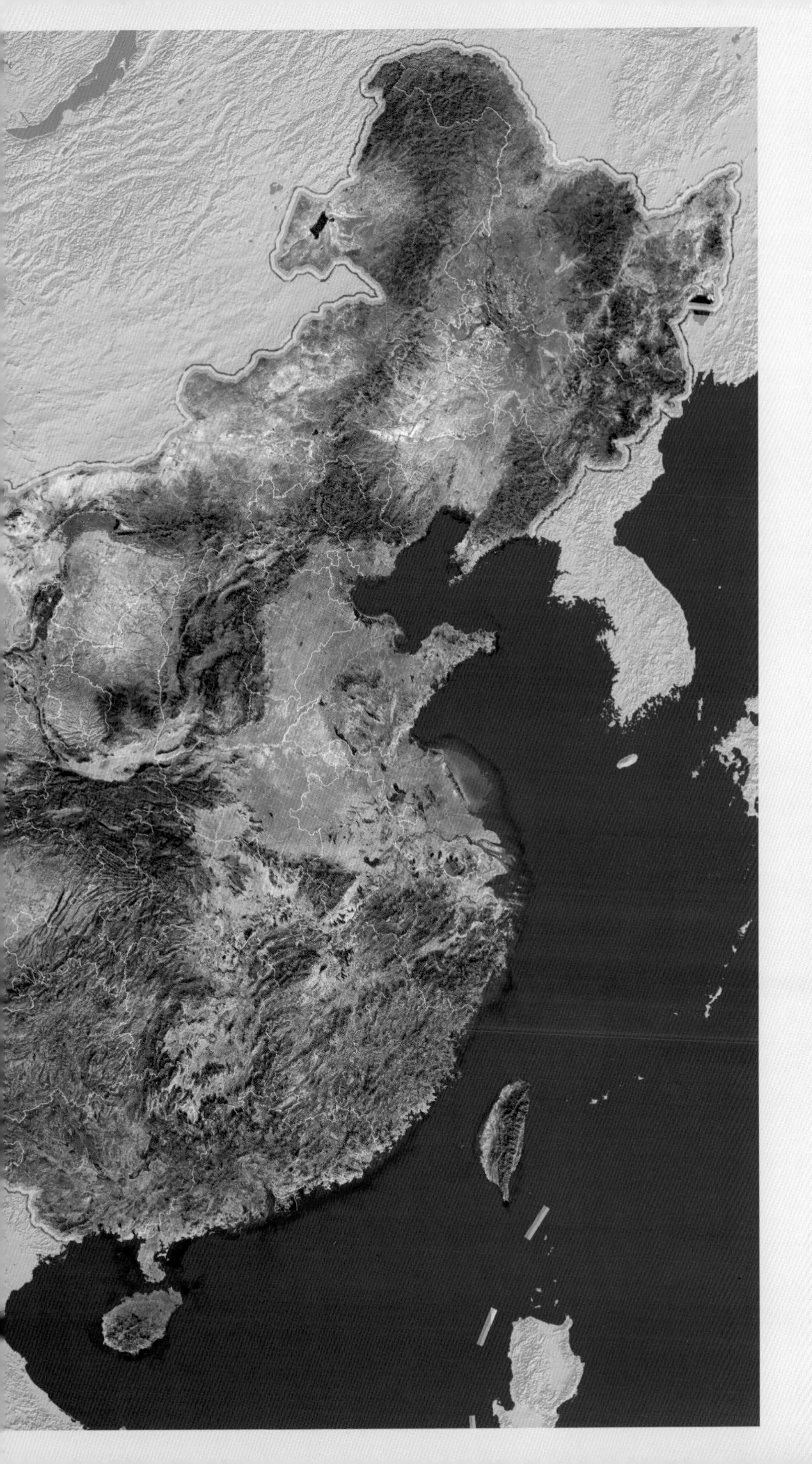

Providers of the photos

Bian Zhiwu
Dong Jing
Hou Heliang
Huang Qian
Liu Xu
Ru Suichu
Wang Chen
Wang Dequan
Wang Rong
Yuan Lianmin
Zhu Enguang
China Foto Press
Quan Jing Photo